BACK ON TOP

BACK ON TOP

The University of Michigan's Odyssey
to the National Championship

GEORGE CANTOR

TAYLOR PUBLISHING COMPANY
DALLAS, TEXAS

Book design by Mark McGarry
Set in Minion

Published by Taylor Publishing Company
1550 West Mockingbird Lane
Dallas, Texas 75235
www.taylorpub.com

Library of Congress Cataloging-in-Publication Data
    Cantor, George, 1941–
      Back on top: the University of Michigan's odyssey to the national
    championship / written by George Cantor.
        p. cm.
    ISBN 0-87833-212-X
    1. University of Michigan—Football—History. 2. Michigan Wolverines (Football
    team)—History. I. Title.
    GV958.U52863C36 1998
    796.332'63'0977435—dc21   98-38639
                                                                          CIP

Printed in the United States of America
10   9   8   7   6   5   4   3   2   1

For Jamie and Courtney:
My favorite Wolverines

CONTENTS

Introduction   *ix*

1   Ann Arbor Pastorale   *1*

2   The Long March   *9*

3   Carr's Choice   *17*

4   Healing the Big Hurt:
September 13. Michigan 27, Colorado 3   *25*

5   Dropping the Torch   *31*

6   Mo's Bad Night   *37*

7   Charles Takes Charge
September 20. Michigan 38, Baylor 3   *45*

8   Starting Over   *53*

9   Lofty Standards   *59*

10   Broom at the Top   *65*

11   Family Ties
September 27. Michigan 21, Notre Dame 14   *71*

12   October 4. Michigan 37, Indiana 0   *77*

13   The Loyalists   *83*

14 October 11. Michigan 23, Northwestern 6   *89*

15 October 18. Michigan 28, Iowa 24   *95*

16 Backyard Brawl   *101*

17 October 25. Michigan 23, Michigan State 7   *107*

18 November 1. Michigan 24, Minnesota 3   *113*

19 Facing Joe Pa   *119*

20 November 8. Michigan 34, Penn State 8   *125*

21 November 15. Michigan 26, Wisconsin 16   *131*

22 We're From O-HIO   *137*

23 November 22. Michigan 20, Ohio State 14   *143*

24 Trophy Time   *151*

25 Bad Numbers   *157*

26 The Subject Was Roses   *165*

27 January 1. Michigan 21, Washington State 16   *171*

28 After the Miracle   *177*

Statistics   *183*

Index   *189*

I was taken to my first game at Michigan Stadium in 1955. I wasn't aware of it at the time, being fourteen years old, but my father and I were in the presence of history. The attendance of 97,366 was the most ever at Michigan. The record would stand for just six weeks, until three more bodies could be squeezed in for the Ohio State game. Army was the opponent, and this also would turn out to be the first time Michigan ever beat them.

In the grainy, old home movies (since converted to tape) my father took of that game, you can make out the grey Corps of Cadets marching in formation across the field. The game action itself is mostly an indiscriminate blur from our seats high in the south end zone. But the view of the stadium, the maize and blue of the uniforms and helmets, the way the bright October sun strikes the turf, that hasn't changed in forty-three years.

Michigan won this game 26-2, and I was eager to see what the authoritative sports columnist H.G. Salsinger, of the *Detroit*

News, would say about it in Sunday's paper. Salsinger was fit to be tied. Late in the game, Bennie Oosterbaan had sent in a third-string quarterback for the last series of downs. He scrambled around on a busted play and wound up getting tackled in his own end zone for a safety.

Salsinger reacted as if the poor kid had been caught handing over atomic secrets to the Russians. "Someone had better inform this young man," he thundered, "that this is not how things are done at Michigan."

That, too, hasn't changed much in forty-three years. The sense of immutable tradition, of upholding the highest standards, of hewing to proper behavior, still permeates everything about Michigan football.

It is not enough simply to win. You must win the Michigan Way.

In 1997, a football team won the Michigan Way. It was a season totally stunning in its surprise and completely satisfying in its denouement. No script could have provided a better cast of characters or a more stirring conclusion.

This book is about that season. It deals with tradition and what it means to play football in Ann Arbor. It is about a program that has won more games than any other in college football, where the past hovers over the present on every Saturday. It is also about how a dynasty almost ended but inexplicably, and without warning, returned to the heights.

"You may never see another season like that," said Bo Schembechler when I interviewed him for this book. "Everything just clicked together. But you may never see another group of players who were so committed to the concept of team."

I spoke to players, coaches, officials, and university administrators while writing this book. But I also wrote about the fans, because they are equally a part of the story. They have packed the stadium to capacity for more than twenty years, followed the team on the road, thrilled to the great moments with their sons and daughters. Their loyalty and devotion to Michigan football is one of the great sagas of college athletics. The championship of the 1997 team was their triumph, too.

"The thing I've enjoyed most about what happened," says linebacker Sam Sword, "is all the people who have come up to me since we won just to thank me. Many of them have tears in their eyes. They just want to tell me how happy we made them feel. That means so much to me. That is the greatest feeling."

I watched the 1998 Rose Bowl with my father. My two daughters, both of whom attend Michigan, sat beside us on the sofa in his apartment. But for a few hours it was like the years had slipped away and I was fourteen again, walking into the big stadium for the first time and thrilling to my first look at Michigan football. Only this time I knew that we were watching history.

GEORGE CANTOR

CHAPTER 1

Ann Arbor Pastorale

Paint me the perfect college town on the last golden Saturday morning of summer. The freeways leading into Ann Arbor already are backed up at the exit ramps. Traffic volumes are building steadily between here and every major city in the state of Michigan. On Main Street through the business district, the line of cars, many of them flying maize and blue banners, can only inch ahead between stoplights.

Those with the foresight to arrive early and beat the rush brush the last crumbs of French toast from the corners of their mouths at Angelo's, or drain the last drop of coffee at The Brown Jug.

They check their watches. Ninety minutes to kickoff.

But no need to know what time it is. On football Saturdays, time stops in Ann Arbor.

In front of the Michigan Union, where John F. Kennedy stood

on the steps late on a campaign night in 1960 and spoke about a new concept he called the Peace Corps, crowds begin to thicken as stadium shuttle buses drop off their passengers. There's not much youthful idealism on view today, however. Instead, young scalpers move easily along the sidewalks, eyes alert for cops, showing off the precious tickets they have to another sold-out stadium.

Across State Street, students stream in from across The Diag, the heart of the campus and the shortest route to the residence halls on The Hill. The crowds moving south on State have turned into a throng, a swelling tide, a vast wave of humanity.

And there is music. At the fraternity houses, Chi Sigma and Beta Theta Pi, parties are going on at full volume. Frat boys and their dates stand on the porches and upper balconies, swaying to the beat. A huge hot air balloon, brought here by a Detroit FM radio station, sits on one of the lawns and the station's live transmission pulsates up and down the street.

One hour to kickoff. But time stands still on football Saturday.

At Hill Street, where the other fraternity and sorority houses are clustered, a second stream flows into the already swollen human tide. Now there is barely room to move on the State Street sidewalk. Past the Taste of Italy and Pizza Bob's and Rod's Diner. Then the long wait for the light at Packard Street. Walkers are swept along like leaves in a flood. "The Victors" blares from an apartment building across the street.

At Hoover comes the start of the sports campus. Within a few blocks are the structures named for those who built the legends. Fielding Yost Arena. Herbert O. Cisler Arena. Don Canham Natatorium. Glenn Schembechler Hall. The names nearly span the twentieth century. No other university comes close to this sort of longevity at the highest level of competition.

There is no longer any space for walking along the sidewalks. The crowds have spilled into the center of Hoover as they swing west. Any driver foolhardy enough to be navigating down this narrow avenue at this time on a football Saturday looks helplessly out his front window as his car is engulfed by the advancing tide.

Suddenly, in front of the James Revelli Building, the crowds part. The University of Michigan Marching Band is taking to the street. A few hundred strong, they come pouring out of the building named for the man who led this band for thirty-six years. They line up across the width of Hoover and blast out a chorus of "The Victors," a song observing its centennial in 1998. It was written by a senior music student, Louis Elbel, who was inspired by a victory over the favored University of Chicago team. Chicago dropped intercollegiate football decades ago, but "The Victors" plays on and on. As the university hastens to remind everyone, no less an authority than John Philip Sousa called it "the finest college march ever written." That was in 1899 and it isn't likely that Sousa changed his mind afterward. The rendition on Hoover Street will be the first of perhaps a hundred times it will be played in the next few hours. As the last notes fade, the band begins moving west, across the railroad tracks and then south on Greene Street.

Now the enormous bulk of the stadium itself is visible at the end of the street. Expanded after the 1997 season, the seventy-one-year-old facility is once more the largest college football stadium in America, leapfrogging past Neyland Field, at the University of Tennessee. The enlargement wasn't solely undertaken as an act of pride, however. The Big House has drawn more than 100,000 spectators for 142 consecutive games. The demand for tickets was so intense in 1997 that freshmen could not obtain them for all the games. Incoming athletic director Tom Goss swore that would never happen again, so three thousand new seats went in.

To the left of the stadium gates is Harry Kipke Drive, named for the coach of Michigan's two undefeated champions of the early 1930s. It leads to a vast lot, open only to season ticket holders. They pay a premium for the privilege of parking close and getting stuck for hours in postgame traffic jams. On football Saturdays it is one huge banquet hall. Tailgate parties are set up from one end of the lot to the other. Footballs and Frisbees are flying everywhere. At the far southwestern corner, on a green patch at the base of the steps leading up to the stadium's eastern gate, is the tent set up by Detroiters Ira Jaffe and Dr. Mel Lester. It is the most elaborate of the pregame spreads. On any given Saturday, under this canopy there will be mountains of bagels, a sea of smoked fish, vats of cheese, vast pools of scrambled eggs, stacks of fruit and veggies, entire tables of cakes and pies. The two friends have been setting up the tent for fifteen years.

"At first it was just for our friends and our kids who were going to school here," explained Jaffe in his downtown Detroit law office. "But then our kids brought their friends, and they brought their friends. How are you going to turn away a hungry college student on a beautiful morning? It's our pleasure to do this for them. Years later I've met some of these kids. And when they hear my name they tell me: 'Oh, I used to come to your tent at the stadium.' How do you put a price on that?"

Now the crowd walks through the outer gates and around the perimeter of the stadium to find the section in which their seats are located. Come too close to kickoff and the line at each entry point can take ten minutes to clear. It takes a while to fit 106,000 people inside.

The voice of Howard King booms from the public address system, as it has since 1972. "Good afternoon, and welcome to the University of Michigan Stadium for this, the fourth meeting between the University of Colorado and Michigan," he says, each word weighted for the proper emphasis.

"It never varies, not by a word," says King. "I think they would lynch me if anything ever changed. That's the way everyone wants it. They don't want change. They want to know that there is, at least, one place on Earth where things go on in their children's day just as it did when their mothers and fathers were here. As many times as I've gone through it, I still have a script in front of me. I'd feel terrible if I dropped a word.

"I feel a tremendous responsibility when I call out the names of these players. I go through the pronunciation over and over again to get it right. I don't even rely on the coaches. Years ago, there was one kid with a tricky name and I went to Bo and asked him how it should be pronounced. He told me and that's what I used. A few weeks later the kid saw me and asked me to pronounce it a different way. 'But that's how Bo said it,' I told him. 'Oh, he's been doing it wrong for three years,' said the kid, 'but I'm afraid to correct him.' So I don't ask the coaches anymore.

"You know that grown men cry when they hear their son's name being announced as playing for Michigan. I owe it to them to get it right," says King.

"Years ago, my predecessor used to announce the scores of the Slippery Rock game. It got to be kind of a gag, I guess, although I didn't catch on at first because I grew up nearby, in eastern Ohio, and knew that Slippery Rock was a pretty good school. But it was another tradition here. When I started doing this, though, they bought a new electronic score service and it just included the major games. So I was stuck. A few times we tried calling the press box at Slippery Rock to get the score, but we didn't always get through. What did I do? I probably shouldn't tell you this, but on a few occasions I just made up a score. Who would know, after all? But we don't do Slippery Rock anymore. That's one tradition we've gotten away from."

But dozens of traditions, big and small, remain. They are in the Ann Arbor air on a football Saturday, when time stops.

Now the marching band comes thundering onto the field. It marches to the north end zone and in a routine that is sacred and inviolable forms the Block M. Then it comes roaring down the field, stepping in unison, roaring out "The Victors." One hundred thousand voices join in the chorus, right hands thrusting into the air at every "Hail" that is sung.

By this time the team is poised at the edge of the tunnel on the east side of the field. At the signal they charge forth, beneath the banner held aloft by letter winners in other sports. "Go Blue," it reads. "M Club Supports You." Every player, coach, and manager leaps up to touch the banner, a touch that binds them to the long, shining history of those who preceded them in this place.

Now we are finally ready for kickoff. The crowd stands again, screaming in anticipation. Another season of Michigan football is about to begin.

There is no richer tradition in the sport. But going into 1997, it appeared that Michigan was foundering, choking under the weight of all this tradition. That the past was too much with this program. That it could not measure up anymore to the standard that had been set before.

One national publication declared the Michigan Dynasty was over and the program was poised to settle back into mediocrity. Outrun and outmuscled by schools inside and outside the Big 10, Michigan clung too firmly to traditions in a rapidly changing world. In trying to maintain the delicate balance of academic and athletic excellence, it was teetering dangerously. One Detroit columnist wrote that he would be "astonished if Michigan ever won another national championship."

Michigan was only a one-point favorite, hardly any margin at all, in its home opener with Colorado, an almost unheard-of situation. The Buffaloes were a fast, talented team with a young, offensive-minded coach, Rick Neuheisel, regarded as being in the vanguard of the sport's new generation. They were expected to challenge Nebraska for the Big 12 title and national honors.

Besides, there was a special resonance to Colorado. It was against Colorado on this very field just three years before that the Michigan program began to come undone. The memory of that game still haunted Michigan fans. So as the big crowd waited for the kickoff to descend, it really had no idea where the ball would be landing this season.

CHAPTER 2

The Long March

Where do you start? Where does this story really begin?

In 1879? That's when Michigan played its first football game, just ten years after Princeton and Rutgers initiated intercollegiate competition in New Brunswick, New Jersey.

In 1901? That's the year Fielding Yost arrived in Ann Arbor and began a streak of fifty-five consecutive games without a loss. His first squad, the famous "Point a Minute" team, outscored the opposition 550-0. For the first time, a university from outside the East Coast was selected as the national champion. That established the tradition.

In 1938? That's when Fritz Crisler came in from Princeton and restored a program that had gone four straight years without a winning record—an unthinkable situation at Michigan. The innovative Crisler brought in the winged helmet, the two-platoon system, a dazzling offensive attack from the single wing. He restored the tradition.

In 1948? That's when Bennie Oosterbaan, building on Crisler's foundation, led the team to a 10-0 season and the undisputed number-one ranking, its first since the Associated Press poll began. That anchored the tradition.

Or was it in 1969? That's when Bo Schembechler was hired out of Miami of Ohio to bring back a program that seemed to have lost its way.

Only eleven times in the twentieth century has a Michigan football team finished with a losing record. Seven of those seasons fell between 1951 and 1967. Only twice in that span did Michigan finish in the Top 10. Only once did it visit the Rose Bowl.

Just as Oosterbaan's successor, Bump Elliott, seemed to have put things back in order, winning eight in a row in 1968, Ohio State humiliated the Wolverines 50-14 in the closing game at Columbus. Michigan accused Woody Hayes of running up the score, going for a two-point conversion to reach the 50 mark. It was the second time in the decade Ohio State had scorched Michigan with that point total and Michigan was 2-7 against Hayes in the 1960s. The Buckeyes finished 1968 as the number-one team in America. There seemed to be no question that it was now the dominant program in the conference. Michigan, although somewhat improved, was not close to competing on even terms. This was an intolerable situation in Ann Arbor.

Among those who watched the annihilation in Columbus was Don Canham, a shrewd businessman with a lot of product to move. His business experience told him that unless your product was better than anyone else's, you were in trouble. Canham also was the newly named athletic director at Michigan, and after that

50-14 pasting, he knew something had to be done. His product was failing. Only once during the season, for the Michigan State game, had the big stadium in Ann Arbor sold out. The other five games on the home schedule averaged 43,000 empty seats. This was no way to run any kind of business.

Canham had already offended the purists by hiring an airplane and having it fly a banner advertising Michigan football over Tiger Stadium, in Detroit. The baseball team was on a pennant run and packing the ball park daily. Canham figured the airborne ad was a great way to reach a larger audience.

"Unless we plan to fill the stadium with shrubbery, we better fill it with people," he explained. "Some of the old-timers did not like to view Michigan football as a commodity. But that's exactly what it is."

Canham devised a mass-mailing campaign, blanketing the state with colorful brochures. To each brochure was attached a coupon for season tickets.

"We touched upon football games, but our real focus was a day on campus," he said. "Tailgate picnics. Cheerleaders. Bands. Spectacle. Things to appeal to all members of the family. The things we had done before to market this program were just not coming off. We had to try something new.

"It wasn't that we were trying to tear down the old Michigan traditions. But you've got to have the hard sell, too. You've got to send out those coupons. You can show how beautiful the stadium looks on television, but when the coupon is sitting right in front of a guy, your chances of a response are immeasurably greater.

"Besides, the whole ball game was changing. The crunch had arrived. The athletic department was unionized, and overnight my expenses went up $120,000. Now I know something about business. I know that if General Motors gets in trouble, it doesn't cut back on Chevrolets. Because that's where the money is. Football was our moneymaker and if that faltered every other program we operated was in trouble."

Canham also knew that he had to give Elliott the ax. A member of the great undefeated 1947 team, the coach was as deeply imbued in Michigan tradition as you can get. He was also an excellent recruiter. Since he had taken over from Oosterbaan in 1959, a succession of outstanding players had come through the Michigan program: Ron Johnson and Dan Dierdorf, Tom Mack and Jack Clancy, Jim Mandich and Tom Keating. They would win individual honors and go on to great professional careers. But they had produced just one conference championship. The word was that Bump was too nice. He was loved by his players, but unable to motivate them to greater achievement.

Within a few weeks of the Ohio State debacle, Elliott was gone. For the first time since Crisler came in thirty-one years before, Michigan would go outside its family to hire a head football coach. The names of the best young coaches in the business—Joe Paterno, Johnny Majors—were floated. Reporters flooded the campus trying to pick up a lead on who the new man would be. Finally, the story was broken by Van Patrick, a veteran Detroit broadcaster who did play-by-play for Notre Dame. He was tipped to it by Ara Parseghian, one of the experts Canham had consulted before making his choice. The new coach would be Schembechler.

To say that Bo was not a household name would be severely understating the situation. Only a few football buffs had ever heard of the man in Michigan. He had been a former assistant to Hayes at OSU and head coach at a tough Mid American Conference school. So many great coaches had come out of Miami—Hayes, Parseghian, Paul Brown, Sid Gillman—that it was called the "Cradle of Coaches." Still, who was this guy? Not only had most Michigan fans never heard his name before, they had no clue how to pronounce it or spell it.

They would learn.

Schembechler's office is located in the building named for him. It is just down the hall and across the corridor from the slightly larger office of head coach Lloyd Carr. Although he has no official job with the university, Schembechler continues to be the essence of Michigan football.

Historian William E. Leuchtenburg wrote a book entitled *In the Shadow of FDR*. Its thesis is that Franklin D. Roosevelt shaped the position of president so profoundly and established the framework of America's political debate so thoroughly, that each of his successors, from Harry Truman to Ronald Reagan, was unavoidably influenced by him. His shadow remained over the White House forty years after his death.

So it is with Bo. His arrival at Michigan in 1969 represented a clear break with an illustrious past that had gone flat. When he coached his last game, at the 1990 Rose Bowl, he left his stamp imprinted on the program. Michigan teams continue in the mold that Schembechler had established. Both Gary Moeller and Carr were his longtime assistants. They studied at the right hand of the master. While the team's style has changed in some particulars it remains, in its essence, within Schembechler's mold.

"It almost looks like I've got a job to go to," he says, waving a visitor into his office. A long meeting had just broken up and his desk is piled high with papers. The meeting concerned an annual charity golf tournament he sponsors in memory of his first wife, Millie, to raise funds for cancer research. It is a job he pursues with the same avidity he brought to coaching. But the demeanor is calmer. After two heart attacks, a frustrating tenure as president of the Detroit Tigers that ended in lawsuits and recriminations, and a good second marriage to a younger woman removed from the football scene, friends say he has mellowed. Well, maybe mellow is not a word that can ever be used in the same sentence as Schembechler. But he seems to be enjoying life.

"That first year, every day at practice we worked on something that we could use to beat Ohio State," he recalls. "Of course, along the way we got creamed by Missouri and knocked off by State—although it was the only time that Duffy (Daugherty) got me. But I knew what the game was.

"I got here at the right time. Look, Bump had recruited some great players and they had gone 8-2 the year before. I wasn't exactly walking into an empty closet. Canham had just taken over and he was a very progressive, forward-looking administrator. Anytime I needed something he never turned me down. Michigan had gone to the Rose Bowl in 1965 and that had been it for a long time. So the situation was right for someone like me."

Those who played for Schembechler in the early years speak now like soldiers who had landed with the third wave at Normandy. It was one of the more terrifying experiences of their lives, but they wouldn't have missed it for anything.

"Awww, I don't think I was that bad," Schembechler says now. "They say I was a screamer. But that's because those practices are so short. You're always working against the clock when you're a college coach. There's never enough time. You have to cram everything you can into a two-hour period. So, yeah, you can't walk up to a player, put your arm around him and say, 'Now son, on that last play maybe it would have been a good idea if you had done it this way.' There's no time for that. You have to let him know in a hurry, and because there's always a lot going on out on the field, you have to let him know loudly. People say that I was hell on wheels back then. But I only did what had to be done.

"They also say that all I could do was run the football. Well, what's so bad about that? I mean if you don't have an offensive line you can't accomplish a thing in a football game. And if you get a unit that can run-block, then you keep doing it until they stop you.

"But the one thing Bump hadn't recruited was a passer. We never had a passing game in those years because we just didn't have the right personnel. Later on, when we had a John Wangler, we threw the football. But when we had great running quarterbacks, Denny Franklin and Rick Leach, we wanted to run it."

On November 22, 1969, Ohio State came into Michigan Stadium as the number-one team in the country, unbeaten in two years. They were ineligible to return to the Rose Bowl. Michigan already had clinched that trip. But the Buckeyes were heavy favorites and Hayes was looking forward to ruining another Michigan season by sending them out to Pasadena with a loss.

What happened that day was one of the most dramatic upsets in college football history and an intrinsic part of Michigan lore. The 24-12 victory changed everything. Never has a program turned around so suddenly and so completely. It was the watershed of modern U-M football. Everything that happened subsequently flowed from that one game and nothing in Ann Arbor would ever be the same again.

CHAPTER 3

Carr's Choice

The crowd of 106,474 for the Colorado game was the seventh largest in Michigan Stadium history. Its size was anticipated but its enthusiasm was puzzling. No one expected much of Michigan this season. Unlike virtually every other year since 1970, Michigan had not been chosen as running one or two for the Big 10 title. In fact, it was slotted in the middle of the pack. Well behind the powerhouses at Penn State and Ohio State. Not quite as good as Iowa. Maybe on a par with the improving Michigan State program, Wisconsin, and Northwestern.

Moreover, Michigan would have to play every one of those schools, as well as Colorado and perennial power Notre Dame, back on the schedule after a lapse of two years. Overall, it may have been the toughest schedule in the school's history. Seven of those teams had been to bowl games the previous year and had won eight or more games. Four were among the top twenty-five winning teams of the '90s.

Middle of the pack. Yeah, just about right.

Carr had not even made his pick for starting quarterback until the last week of practice. It would be fifth-year senior Brian Griese instead of the previous season's starter, Scott Dreisbach. This, too, contributed to a general sense of unease about this team.

Griese's career had been uneven at best. He had come to Michigan as a walk-on, after being heavily recruited by his father's school, Purdue. The younger Griese knew in West Lafayette the comparisons with Bob Griese would have been inevitable. The elder Griese had taken Purdue to its only Rose Bowl, in 1967, and then led the Miami Dolphins to three Super Bowls. His place in the Hall of Fame rested on a secure base of accomplishment. No matter how well the son played, how could he ever compare to the father?

It was one of the same reasons Peyton Manning gave for choosing Tennessee over his father Archie's alma mater, Mississippi. Peyton, however, had established a great career of his own and was now regarded as the top college quarterback in the country. The Volunteers were mentioned as possible national champions. While Manning had been the most heavily recruited prospect of his year, Griese's contact with Michigan was limited to a visit at his Florida home by head coach Gary Moeller. He apologized for running out of scholarships before getting to Brian. But he added that if he came in as a walk-on and made the team, maybe something could be arranged. Griese, an excellent student, was attracted by Michigan's academic reputation. That was good enough for his father. He told his son that if Michigan was what he wanted, he would pay the tuition.

Griese made the team but was passed over as a junior in favor of Dreisbach, a sophomore, for the starting job. When Dreisbach went down with a thumb injury in the second half of the 1995 season, Griese got his chance. But the following year, as a senior, he was a backup again. Average arm, said the rap sheet. Good head, but underwhelming tools. Griese was relegated for most of the year to "pootsch kicking," coming in to punt when Michigan had the ball near midfield to try and kick it out of bounds inside the 10. Griese had a talent for it. But it was a far cry from a quarterback's dream. He had resigned himself to passing up his final year of eligibility and going ahead to graduate school.

But with thirty minutes left in his football career, it all turned around. Playing in Columbus against undefeated Ohio State, Michigan was down 9-0 at the half. With Dreisbach again hobbled with injuries, Griese came in. At the start of the third quarter, on a second and nine play at his own 31, he hit Tai Streets on a quick slant across the middle. Defensive back Shawn Springs slipped for an instant on the turf and that was all Streets needed. He ran the 69 yards for a touchdown. Michigan went on to control the rest of the game behind Griese and won 13-9.

The loss cost Ohio State its shot at a national championship, pleasure enough in itself in Ann Arbor. It also placed Griese in the starter's role in the Outback Bowl against Alabama. He again played well. But he also threw an interception in the fourth quarter that was returned 88 yards for a touchdown, the margin of victory in the 17-14 Alabama win. Until spring practice he was still convinced that the wisest course was to get on with his life and give up on football.

Then he abruptly changed his mind, took command in the preseason drills, and here he was. The quarterback job was his as a fifth-year senior. Even as he took the field against Colorado, some Michigan supporters and media felt he would not keep it long. Before the season progressed much farther, they said, the job would belong to Tom Brady, a sophomore in eligibility with the best arm on the team. Given the difficulty of the schedule and Griese's inability to throw long consistently, it had to happen.

Middle of the pack. Just about right.

Then there was the problem of the offensive line. This was the hallmark of all the great teams in the Schembechler era and beyond. Everything flowed from the ability to control the ball. Bo said it was the first element for which he recruited: first the offensive line, then the defensive line, and only then the skill players.

This offensive line was far too young by Michigan standards. Zach Adami and Jon Jansen were the only returning interior linemen with proven abilities and Adami was being asked to play out of position, at center. Jeff Backus, a redshirt freshman, was trying to come back from a ruptured appendix suffered the previous winter. He had dropped thirty-seven pounds during the ordeal, and there was some question if he had been able to sufficiently build up his strength. Other jobs were being contested for by sophomores and redshirts. This line was a work in progress and probably would not come together until midway in the season, if then.

The defensive front had more experience and was one of the fastest ever put together at Michigan. But the questions here were about weight and strength. Glen Steele was solid at defensive end as a senior. But there were doubts whether the rest of the line would be able to keep offensive linemen off Michigan's talented corps of linebackers. This group was regarded as a positive, but to be effective it had to get room. This was a concern.

The team's unquestioned strength was its defensive backfield. Anchored by All-American Charles Woodson, it was a veteran unit that played with fearless bravado. But if the line was over-powered and the linebackers unable to exert consistent pressure, even the best defensive backs could hold coverage for only so long. The entire defensive unit had played well through the 8-4 season in 1996, looking shaky only in the 29-17 loss to Penn State. Defensive coordinator Jim Herrmann was enthusiastic, innovative, and had a knack for getting his players to sign on with some of his ideas. Still it didn't look much like a Michigan defense from the vintage years.

Middle of the pack. Just about right.

And then there was the coach.

Nice guy, Lloyd Carr. Grew up in the Detroit downriver suburb of Riverview. An all-state quarterback, he went to college at Northern Michigan. He came home to coach high school football in Belleville and Westland and serve as president of the Riverview Board of Education. Solid citizen. Joined the Michigan staff in 1980. Keeps Placido Domingo tapes on his car stereo; enjoys golf, reading, and breakfast at Angelo's. Favorite book is *Man's Search for Meaning*. One of the few football coaches who is also a political liberal.

But he keeps losing four games a year.

Carr never sought the spotlight. Although he interviewed for the Wisconsin head coaching job in 1989, he seemed content at Michigan, an institution that attracted him, he said, because of its traditions and its standards. He arrived a day late at his first Big 10 head coaches meeting, and since everyone else had been interviewed the previous day, he was the sole target of the media when he got there. He told Michigan's then sports information director, Bruce Madej, that it was the most uncomfortable experience of his life. "And if we're lucky, we'll do it again next year," Madej responded. Carr knew what he meant and laughed.

He couldn't bring himself to use Gary Moeller's space in the parking lot for weeks after he replaced him as head coach. It took even longer for Carr to move into Moeller's vacant office. When Harry Truman suddenly learned that he had replaced Franklin D. Roosevelt as president, his response was: "I felt as if the sun, moon, and stars had all fallen on me." Carr acted the same way. It was the last thing he thought could happen. When the announcement was made the first thing he did, tears in his eyes, was to defend Moeller, his longtime friend.

Loyal, steadfast, and true. That was Lloyd Carr.

But he keeps losing four games a year.

In most sports, at most places, a .667 winning percentage is splendid. But not with Michigan football. In Ann Arbor, .667 is a ticket out.

"I never heard the boos when I was an assistant coach," Carr says. "Only once, when we were undefeated and ran off the field at the half against Illinois leading 7-6. And they booed us. I couldn't believe it at the time.

"But now I tell the kids I recruit that Michigan is not for everybody. I tell them it's hard here. You have to give a lot to succeed. You have to know how to embrace the pressure and make it a positive thing. Expectations are very high every year. Anything less than a Rose Bowl is considered a failure. When you coach here it doesn't take long to learn how high those standards are. When you win, it's expected. When you lose....Sure I heard the grumbling. All those four-loss seasons. You couldn't not hear it. But, hey, every job has its drawbacks."

It had been a difficult run up to this season for him. While he was preparing his team for the Outback Bowl, his seventy-five-year-old mother, Pauline, had been diagnosed with cancer. Carr moved her into his Ann Arbor home and spent the last five months of his mother's life with her.

"It was a wonderful and, at the same time, a very sad time," he says, "because in those five months we had a lot of good times together. We had some great conversations. In the midst of this pain, she still maintained the fight and concern for other people. I would hope that I could be as strong as she was.

"But as for the job, you don't ever get away from it. I don't think there's ever a minute when I stop being a football coach. That's one of the things that happens to you in this job."

But if Carr knew any secrets about his team as he began his third full season as Michigan's head coach, he wasn't letting on. As far as anyone knew, another four-loss season did not seem out of the question. And as things go at Michigan, it could have been Carr's last.

CHAPTER 4

Healing the Big Hurt
September 13. Michigan 27, Colorado 3

Colorado never knew what hit 'em.

They went three and out on their first series of downs. When they got the ball back, their first two plays from scrimmage lost three yards. Then quarterback John Hessler went back to pass from his own 28. With Wolverines coming at him from every angle, he turned the ball loose. Charles Woodson was waiting to gather it in.

First turnover of the year. Hessler left the field looking stunned and Michigan drove right in for a touchdown.

"You could see the kids were like 'Wow,'" says Jim Herrmann. "They were thinking, 'Hey, if we do what we're supposed to do, this is what's going to happen.'"

Carr later called this series of downs the advance indicator of how the entire season would go. "I think our defense really caught the imagination of the fans," he says. "Our crowd adopted that defense. Our team fed off that enthusiasm in all those big games we played at home."

"We had been practicing all week during two-a-days, saying that we wanted to be vicious, to hit their quarterback hard, and stop them all," said Woodson. "The defense on this team wanted to make things happen. Every time he let the ball go we were in his face and we were hitting him and putting him in the dirt. Any time a quarterback goes through pressure like that, sooner or later he's going to throw some bad balls."

High above the field in his own box, Bo Schembechler saw what was happening and began to think bright thoughts. "Lloyd didn't have the personnel before that could make the big negative plays," he said. "When I saw them get after their quarterback like that, I knew that something interesting was happening."

With blitzes coming at him from every side of the field and from every defensive position, Hessler came unglued. He had confessed to being nervous in the previous week's game, his first as a starter, a narrow win over underdog Colorado State. This was more than a case of nerves. This was collapse. He threw three more interceptions and never managed to mount anything resembling an offense.

In former years, Michigan fans had been accused of being undemonstrative, of sitting back and waiting for something to happen before they got into games. But something was sure happening now. The old bend-but-don't break defensive concept was out the window. Michigan was attacking, forcing the other team to react to them. The crowd loved it.

"That Colorado game set the tone for the whole season," says linebacker Sam Sword. "There is no better feeling than attacking, blitzing. There was the mentality of, 'All right, let's get after them.'

"But you can't play that defense unless you believe in each other. Every man has to know that everyone else is going to do their job. We had to stick together to make it work. What I really liked is that just when they were convinced we were coming with another blitz, we'd drop back into zone coverage and the quarterback had no idea where to go with the ball. You could see it in their eyes. They didn't know how to beat us."

"We got our tails whipped," said Neuheisel afterward. "They were all over me," said Hessler, who was red-eyed following a postgame conference with his coach.

Almost overlooked in the defensive eruption was the calm precision of Griese. He was 21 of 28 passing with two touchdowns and continually, methodically hit his tight end, Jerame Tuman, on short patterns off play-action sequences. Colorado reacted as if this simple play was something new and startling and Griese kept coming back to it.

"Brian didn't force anything," said Carr. "He was smart. I think you're going to see a better quarterback than he's given credit."

Early in the fourth quarter it was all over, the traffic-beaters already were making their way out of the stadium. It was quite a contrast to the previous two meetings between the schools. In 1996, Michigan had beaten the Buffaloes in Boulder 20-13. The game wasn't decided until Koy Detmer's final pass from the Michigan 38 in the last seconds was swatted down.

But that was only a faint echo of the 1994 game, one of the most devastating losses in Michigan's history. It can be marked as another turning point for the school, as much of a watershed in its own way as the famous 24-12 win over Ohio State in 1969. Three years later, the cloud left by this game still darkened perceptions of the Michigan team and was probably as instrumental as anything else in the chain of events that led to Gary Moeller's dismissal as head coach the following spring.

Ranked number four in the country at the time and considered a top Rose Bowl choice, Michigan thoroughly outplayed Colorado for three and a half quarters, holding a three-touchdown lead. Quarterback Kordell Stewart then begin rallying his team. When Colorado got the ball back for the last time, it still trailed 26-21. There were only seconds to play and the Buffs were 64 yards from the goal. Stewart's desperation pass was batted around in the end zone by Michigan defenders, but far too carelessly. As the big crowd watched in disbelief, the pass bounced high in the air and then plopped easily into the waiting arms of Detroit-born receiver Michael Westbrook as time expired. It was one of the most exciting endings to any game in football history. It absolutely crushed the Michigan team.

"I was standing on the sidelines and saying, 'Yeah, we're going to the national championship,'" says senior safety Marcus Ray, who was then a redshirt freshman. "We were number four and the schedule was favorable. When I saw that play, I was hurt. I was heartbroken. I was crying."

More than that, the game exposed glaring weaknesses in the Michigan defense. The team surrendered 268 points that season, more than 22 a game, the most given up by any Michigan team.

Just like Pearl Harbor, Michigan fans still remember where they were when the bomb fell.

"I was out in California getting ready for a wedding," recalls Dr. Marshall Golden, of Minnetonka, Minnesota. "I had been downstairs with a friend watching the game on TV and when everything seemed to be under control I went back to the room to shower and dress. The TV was on and I was shaving when they flashed the final score. I almost cut my throat. At that very instant, the phone rang and it was the guy I'd been watching the game with. He was so stunned he could barely get the words out."

For those close to the Michigan program, the shock was much worse than that. It seemed to drain the spirit and confidence from the entire team, coaches and players alike. If you couldn't protect that lead on your own field, what lead was safe?

In terms of points, it was not the worst defeat that a Moeller-coached team had suffered in Michigan. In 1991, his second year on the job, Florida State came into Ann Arbor and mauled the Wolverines, 51-31. It was the most points given up by a Michigan team since Ara Parseghian's Northwestern ran up 55 on them in 1958, the most scored against them at Michigan Stadium in history. The Seminoles dug up little patches of hallowed Michigan turf to bury in a special stadium plot in Tallahassee where road wins are commemorated. Michigan fans could do nothing but seethe. For one of the few times in recent seasons, it was clear Michigan had lost to a clearly superior team. Florida State was ranked number one at the time, and Michigan simply could not match its speed on either side of the ball. They were flying past the Wolverine blockers and tacklers.

But Moeller learned from the experience. Recruiting patterns were changed. To compete on a national level, to get faster, it was clear Michigan would have to move well beyond its traditional territory around the Great Lakes.

"When I got to Michigan, it was almost entirely a team from our state, Ohio, and the Chicago area," recalls Schembechler. "For those times, that was enough. We didn't go into the South too much and only rarely to California or New England. Anthony Carter was really the first great player from Florida that we brought in, and that was becoming the top state in the country for skilled talent."

But by 1997, Michigan recruiting had cast a far wider net. There were eighteen players on the team from Florida, Texas, and California, compared to twenty-one from the traditional areas of Ohio, Indiana, and Illinois. Griese had grown up in Florida. His tight end, Tuman, was from Kansas, and starting flanker Russell Shaw from Los Angeles. Running backs Chris Howard and Chris Floyd were both recruited out of Louisiana, while top quarterback prospect Tom Brady also came from California.

Along the offensive line, Zach Adami was from Arkansas, Jeff Backus from Georgia, and Steve Hutchinson from Florida. On the defense were Juaquin Feazell from Georgia, Ben Huff from North Carolina, Rob Swett from Pennsylvania, Daydrion Taylor from Texas, and Dhani Jones from Maryland.

Lesson learned. The players Moeller recruited after the Florida State drubbing, and the areas his staff opened up for Michigan, supplied much of the core of the 1997 team.

But he would not be there to see it.

CHAPTER 5

Dropping the Torch

It was inevitable that he would be compared to Bo. Even his nickname, Mo, was a reminder. Gary Moeller was the master's chosen disciple. He had played for Schembechler, who was an assistant coach when Moeller captained the 1962 Ohio State team. Then he coached on Bo's staff at Miami and came with him to Ann Arbor. Moeller functioned as an assistant head coach until being offered the top job at Illinois in 1977. But he won only six games in three years, none against Michigan, and was fired, despite outspoken protests by his players. Moeller stated that alumni groups wanted to take recruiting shortcuts he could not tolerate. "If you want to build a fast program and panic, then you can go out and cheat and get it," he said. Moeller was no cheater.

He rejoined Bo in 1980, bringing with him Lloyd Carr, who had been an assistant at Illinois. The succession was thus established. Schembechler, competitive against all teams, felt a special enmity toward Illinois for what he regarded as unfair treatment of his protégé. Moeller was not given enough time to rebuild a program that was in shambles, although regarded by most Big 10 observers, including Don Canham, as "a sleeping giant." He still refers to Moeller's successor, Mike White, as a "cheater" and is convinced that he bent the rules to bring in ineligible transfers. White also employed a wide-open passing attack, which Bo regarded as effete. He seemed to take special delight in destroying White's Illinois teams, racking up 70 points against them in 1981 and 69 points in 1986.

Some, however, said part of Mo's trouble at Illinois was that he could never shake Michigan from his mind. His assistant coach Glen Mason, now the head coach at Minnesota, recalls Moeller's first home opener with the Illini. "He got up and said, 'We are going to play with enthusiasm and emotion. We are going to make these fans proud. When this game is over, they'll throw the biggest party Ann Arbor ever saw!'"

As Moeller stopped, says Mason, the players stirred and one of them finally said, "Coach, it's Champaign."

"Champagne," said Moeller furiously. "Hell, no. There'll be no champagne after this game. That's not how we celebrate."

Moeller coached the Michigan team to a last-second comeback win against Alabama in the 1988 Hall of Fame Bowl while Schembechler was recovering from bypass surgery. When Bo finally decided to step down as coach, after taking the athletic director's job, he echoed what his predecessor, Canham, had said twenty years before. "You must understand that the financial stability of the entire athletic department depends on the continuity and success of the football program," he said. "I will do everything in my power to make sure this program is run the right way."

That said, the choice was inevitable. Moeller knew the program from the inside out. "I wanted a man who thinks like I do, who believes in the Michigan system," Bo added at the formal announcement of the hiring, just before the 1990 Rose Bowl.

Moeller came in with a reputation of being a slightly less scary version of Bo. There was always an element of intimidation in Schembechler's coaching techniques. He says now that "the success of my program was that I gave every man on my teams, from the top stars to the hundredth guy on the roster, a meaningful job to do. I always made it clear that the guys who only got on the field at practice were just as important in my mind and were just as vital to the team as the ones who started on Saturday."

That may be true in Bo's mind. But many of his former players thought the coach, so encrusted in legend, had become inaccessible, unapproachable in later years to all but a few. When he became president of the Detroit Tigers the confrontational style he favored in a college setting did not win him many admirers in the wider world. His refusal to compromise on demands for a new ball park to replace aging Tiger Stadium ("You cannot chain us a to a rusting girder."), and his acquiescence to the firing of beloved announcer Ernie Harwell, won him negative media for the first time in Michigan. And when he was fired by owner Tom Monaghan in 1992, days before the ball club was sold, Schembechler responded with a civil suit against his former employer and an uncharacteristic public airing of his grievances.

Moeller wanted to change some of that style. "I can't be like Bo; that's not me," he said upon taking the job. "This program will have a lot of Bo Schembechler in it, without question. But it will be Gary Moeller's program. People think I'm softer in some ways than Bo, but I don't think I am. I think I have a longer point to where I boil, but when I get mad, I stay mad.

"Maybe I have a little more patience with players. I'd rather coach from a positive approach, get a kid fired up. You've got to give them some confidence and make them a dominant player, mentally and physically."

But Jerry Hanlon, an assistant coach with both men, grinned slyly and said: "One letter, that's the difference. From B to M. Sure, Gary's different from Bo. He's trying to develop his own personality and how we wants to be perceived. But I don't think his program will be any different."

National television analyst Beano Cook predicted, however, that Moeller would last no more than three to five years on the job. "I hope I'm wrong," he said, "but judging on what Bo did and what he did at Illinois, I don't see it. He may last five because Michigan isn't as bloodthirsty as some schools."

It started well. Inheriting a loaded team from Bo, Moeller took it to a 9-3 record in 1990. But two of the defeats came in the last two minutes and a 28-27 loss to Michigan State is still considered a stolen win in Ann Arbor. A non-call on blatant pass interference in the end zone on a two-point conversion attempt after the clock had run out was the final margin.

Moeller won his last six straight, finished with a flourish over Ohio State and a Gator Bowl stomping of Mississippi, and wound up seventh in the Associated Press (AP) poll. The team started 1991 ranked second, survived the Florida State slaughter, and went to the Rose Bowl, where an outstanding Washington team (national champions in the CNN/USA Today poll) beat them soundly. Michigan was ranked sixth.

In 1992 they didn't lose a game, although consecutive ties to Illinois and Ohio State at the end of the season did dampen enthusiasm. But they ran over Washington in a return trip to Pasadena, 38-31, and moved up one notch in the ranking, to number five.

So in his first three years, the low end of Cook's longevity pre-
diction, Moeller went 28-5-3, matching a standard worthy of
Schembechler. Within the Big 10 he was 20-2-2, racking up nineteen straight victories (a conference record) and twenty-one
games without a loss.

But in 1993 the program hit a bump. It went just 8-4, with
losses to Michigan State and a last-minute giveaway to Illinois on
a fumble.

In 1994 came the morale-sapping loss to Colorado. Moeller
insisted a home defeat three weeks later by Penn State, the even-
tual Big 10 champion, hurt more. But Michigan turned up excep-
tionally flat in losses to Wisconsin and Ohio State. In no game
could it hold opponents to fewer than two touchdowns. Its bowl
was the lackluster Holiday where it handled Western Athletic
Conference champ Colorado State easily enough. But no one was
waving banners over that. The ranking in the AP poll fell to
twelfth.

This was the end of Moeller's fifth season at Michigan and the
grumbling had now reached a steady roar. During
Schembechler's twenty-one years Michigan had lost as many as
four games only four times, and never in consecutive years. Now
it was two straight. Uncomplimentary letters poured into the
Michigan athletic department offices. The anonymous voices of
sports talk radio mauled Moeller viciously. Pictures of him
wearing a dunce cap circulated around campus. The pressure on
him was growing dangerously, to a point few coaches at few institutions would ever know. Carr tells his recruits that "Michigan
isn't for everybody." But that applies to coaches as well as players.

"I can't pretend I'm tougher than nails and it doesn't bother
me," Moeller told *Detroit News* columnist Bob Wojnowski that
year. "I'm an adult and I can deal with it. But it isn't right.

"Everyone wants to be Number One. That's what the whole

world focuses on—who is the best? Well, I want to be Number One, but it's not easy. And you have to do it the proper way. But God dang when you go out there and try your damndest and sometimes you don't win, what can you do?"

Joe Falls, a journalistic institution in the state, called Michigan fans "spoiled rotten." "Try giving Michigan State the U-M record under Moeller and see what the reaction would be," he wrote. "You hear whispers of discipline problems but nobody ever comes forward and puts their name on what these problems are. It's always easy to whisper. I just think he is getting a bad rap. I believe there is more to athletics than winning or losing."

Moeller admitted that the team may have not been ready to play against Wisconsin, but was simply overpowered by Ohio State. "We were much higher for that game than we were when we went down there two years ago and got tied," he said. "I think we were a darn good football team but we had a couple pieces that didn't fall in place for us that we were counting on. As a coach, you take responsibility for that. When you're playing in front of people, you have to be the guy who goes home undefeated. Media has really put us in a difficult situation. It blows your mind sometimes."

Moeller gave that interview in late December, as his team was preparing for the Holiday Bowl. It was the last game he would coach at Michigan. Four months later, the pressure grew too great to withstand.

CHAPTER 6

Mo's Bad Night

The night of April 28, 1995, began as a quiet Friday evening out for Moeller and his wife, Ann. They chose Excalibur, a pricey restaurant in the Detroit suburb of Southfield, about a forty-five-minute drive from the Michigan campus. The restaurant had gained fame because Frank Sinatra admired its ribs and subsequently it attracted a quasi-celebrity clientele. What happened there that evening turned it into a landmark of a different sort—such as Machus' Red Fox, about four miles away, where Jimmy Hoffa disappeared twenty years before.

According to eyewitness accounts, the Moellers finished dinner, but the Michigan coach continued to drink heavily. He began singing loudly with the musical group, flirting with waitresses, banging glasses on the table. When the glasses were removed he continued to hammer away with his coffee cups and salt and pepper shakers, until they, too, had to be taken away. His wife, mortified, urged him to leave, and when he refused she went out to sit in the car. Other patrons began to complain, and Moeller grabbed one man near his table by the lapels. When the night manager approached, Moeller poked him in the chest repeatedly and refused requests to have a cab called for him.

At most first-class restaurants, incidents involving well-known guests are hushed up to avoid embarrassment. Excalibur managers felt they had no alternative but to call the police. Officer Vincent Maviglia was first to arrive on the scene. According to his report, and those of other police officials, he found Moeller in the parking lot, demanding profanely to re-enter the restaurant. His wife was still in the family car, but Moeller was clearly in no condition to drive. Two police sergeants then arrived at the scene and one of them saw Moeller swearing at Maviglia and poking him in the chest. Warned repeatedly not to attack the officers, Moeller refused and challenged them to arrest him. The officers now felt they had no option but to arrest him for disorderly conduct and assaulting a police officer.

He was taken to the Oakland County Jail, but because his intoxication level was so high authorities turned him away. Police drove him, instead, to Providence Hospital, in Southfield. He had to be taken to the trauma room, separate from other patients, because of the abuse he kept shouting at police and hospital personnel. Finally, on Saturday morning he was booked and sent home.

The story broke the following day, but it didn't spiral out of control until Monday. When it was learned that Southfield officers use audio recorders in their encounters with citizens, several local media outlets requested a copy of the tape under the state's Freedom of Information Act. Part of the transcript ran in both daily newspapers. But it was the sound of the outburst, run repeatedly (some would say mercilessly) on Detroit radio and television, that was the crowning blow. It was one thing to see the statements in type, quite another to hear the drunken outbursts, the shouting and screaming. Several morning radio shows that cater to a subliterate male audience took enormous relish in replaying the tapes for days. "It's all over for you," he yelled at the officers. "I'll beat the shit out of you. You know what you are? You're a fucking coward. You know I haven't done anything wrong. You love it, you big chickens."

Later, Moeller became remorseful, practically sobbing. "You won't let me go. I understand why you can't let me go. I don't want my kids to see me this way."

On Tuesday he was suspended as head coach, to be replaced by his top assistant, Lloyd Carr. On Thursday he resigned, although subsequent documents revealed he was fired after refusing to accept athletic director Joe Roberson's offer of a year-long leave of absence "to sort out his problems." Despite the fact that Roberson had said earlier that "he's not going to lose his job" and admitted no complete investigation of the incident had been made, Moeller was out. He had lasted five years, just as Beano Cook had predicted in 1989.

It seemed inexplicable. Here was a man who had functioned with never a breath of impropriety. A great family man, a model of moral rectitude. It was not only out of character, it sounded insane. Moeller was the last man anyone expected to blow. "It's like he was possessed or something," said his quarterback, Todd Collins. "It seems like he had a rage that night."

Observers of Michigan football felt Moeller might have had a desire to control more than he possibly could. Joe Falls wrote, tellingly, that if he was coming off an 11-1 season instead of two straight 8-4 years, the outcome might have been different. But even sympathizers knew how difficult it would be for Moeller to resume his job as football coach and regain his stature as a guide to proper behavior.

Even longtime rivals were stunned. "This speaks to the pressures that are on college football coaches," said Ohio State's John Cooper, who had saved his job by managing to tie Moeller's team in 1992. "It reinforces that if some people are out there to get you, you can't give them an excuse."

"All I know is it's a lousy deal," said George Perles, former Michigan State coach. "I wish he could have a second chance. Everybody deserves a second chance."

To which Roberson responded: "Second chances are somewhat dependent on what the circumstances were that caused you to lose the first chance."

Some thought that if Schembechler had intervened with Roberson, Moeller's job might have been saved. But Bo was on an extended fishing trip to Mexico. By the time he returned to Ann Arbor, there was little he could do.

There was much more happening under the surface. Michigan had always prided itself on its unblemished athletic image. Things were supposed to be done the Michigan Way. You not only were expected to win, you had to win with class.

In the '90s, however, things had started to unravel. Irregularities in the baseball program brought in a new coach, former Detroit Tigers' catcher Bill Freehan, to save it. Hockey coach Red Berenson was booked for urinating in public. Two of Moeller's players were thrown off the team for stealing beer. Another one fired a shot at police officers in the mistaken belief that they were thieves trying to steal his car. Three more players admitted to stealing a credit card and buying merchandise with it. This was shocking behavior. Someone had to be held responsible.

The biggest upheaval was in the basketball program after the arrival of the Fab Five at Ann Arbor in 1991. They were the most highly touted freshman basketball class gathered by any college in recent years. These players crowned the recruiting career of coach Steve Fisher. He had stepped into the basketball job under unlikely circumstances. Before the 1989 NCAA playoffs, former coach Bill Frieder revealed he had accepted the job as head coach at Arizona State for the next season. Schembechler, acting in his capacity as athletic director, promptly dismissed Frieder, saying he wanted the team to be coached in the tournament "by a Michigan man." That meant Fisher, the top assistant, who had never held a head coaching job before. His star-packed team swept through six straight victories to give Michigan its first basketball championship in history. (Only three schools ever have won both an NCAA basketball title and an AP football championship—Michigan, Michigan State, and Ohio State.)

Fisher, like Carr in six more years, was not the university's first choice as the permanent head coach. It would have preferred a bigger name. Moreover, there had always been tension between the football and basketball programs. Despite outstanding teams, and three trips to the Final Four in the '60s and '70s, basketball coaches felt themselves to be castoff stepchildren, far below football in the Michigan pecking order. The situation led Frieder's predecessor, John Orr, to resign and take the job at Iowa State. Now Frieder, feeling the same frustration, also resigned.

The university was stuck with Fisher. How do you fire an undefeated coach who had just won a championship? After two indifferent years, he came up with the Fab Five. As freshmen, they went all the way to the NCAA finals before losing to defending champion Duke. The Fabs were a national sensation. Their midcalf shorts were copied by youngsters around the country and their trash-talking on the court turned into a craze. But to Old Blues, this was not the way it was done at Michigan. To them the Fab Five were a source of concern, an embarrassment in waiting. When it was revealed that some of them had accepted payments of several hundred dollars to appear at a charity event, a fundraiser for medical research, in outstate Michigan, there were cries of outrage. It was pointed out in their defense that these were kids from poor families who needed spending money. Their scholarships covered all their college expenses, but still left them with no cash. But even a second trip to the Final Four, ending in a loss in the finals to North Carolina, didn't quiet the critics. And when Chris Webber turned pro after only his sophomore year, the sense of disquiet deepened.

Their success had turned Michigan into a national basketball power. But there was a steep downside. All of this was on the minds of university administrators when Moeller stepped over the line. The accumulation of problems on all the athletic teams landed, justly or not, on Moeller's head.

Less than a year after Moeller's firing, several of Fisher's players and recruit Mateen Cleaves were in a utility vehicle that flipped over on the freeway between Detroit and Ann Arbor. It was long after hours; the recruit had been taken an impermissible distance off campus under the NCAA rules, and there was some question about what a college player was doing driving a $30,000 automobile. The investigation into this and other incidents, involving payments to players by a booster, led to Fisher's dismissal immediately before the start of the 1997–98 season. In a strange repeat of Moeller's firing, Fisher was never accused of anything specific. But he hadn't done things the Michigan Way.

Moeller still refuses to speak about the incident that cost him the job he cherished. "That's all behind me now," is all he will say.

"It's a closed book." Closet psychiatrists have examined the incident exhaustively. Rumors about other hushed-up run-ins with police in Ann Arbor occasionally surface, but have never been verified. It seems clear, though, that Cooper had it right. The pressures on big-time college coaches have grown unbearable. As bad as they are at Michigan, they are far worse at places like Alabama, Texas, and Notre Dame.

"When you arrive at Notre Dame," former coach Lou Holtz used to say, "they tell you that the wins don't matter. Just run a clean, competitive program. But when you go 8-3, they want to know why you weren't in a major bowl. When you go 10-1 they want to know why you weren't number one. And when you're 11-0 they want to know why you're not blowing everybody out. It never stops."

Moeller signed as an assistant coach with the Cincinnati Bengals, on the recommendation of Schembechler, for the 1995 season. A year later he moved to Detroit to become linebackers coach for the Lions. That enabled him to keep his home in Ann Arbor and commute to the Lions operation in Pontiac, an hour away.

"This football program is wounded and it is in great pain," said Carr, tears of anger in his eyes, on the day he was named to replace Moeller, the close friend who had brought him to Michigan. "But we don't want your tears and we don't want your sorrow. We have a program of kids with great character, great courage, and a great will to win. Michigan will be back."

CHAPTER 7

Charles Takes Charge
September 20. Michigan 38, Baylor 3

Even before a single down of the season was played this looked to be the one soft spot on the Michigan schedule. No traditional rivalry here. No intersectional grudge match. Baylor and Michigan had played only once before, in 1975, when the Bears were coming off a Cotton Bowl appearance. The game ended 14-14.

Michigan over the years had, in fact, very little to do with the old Southwestern Conference (Baylor's former affiliation before moving to the Big 12). Michigan had only played three other teams from that defunct organization. The Wolverines never met its two major powers, Texas or Arkansas. Nor, for that matter, have they ever played several other southern powers. Louisiana State and Florida, Clemson and Tennessee—all of them historic programs with national championships in their trophy cases. The school from outside the Midwest that Michigan has played most often is Penn. They met twenty-one times, but not since 1953 when the Quakers decided to de-emphasize football.

In the 1990s, Michigan's schedulers attempted to renew some old rivalries and move beyond its regional base. There were first-ever meetings with Boston College, Houston, and Memphis. Michigan played Schembechler's old school, Miami, for the first time in seventy-one years. In 1998 it will meet Syracuse for the first time in eighty years and Eastern Michigan, its Washtenaw County neighbor, will come down the road to play for the first time since 1931. Some of that, however, was a deliberate attempt at downsizing the schedule. There was a belated realization that a brutal lineup of games, such as in 1997, could only hurt the team's chances for a championship. If Michigan loses to a ranked team while Nebraska and Florida State sweep aside any number of pushovers, comparative schedules don't seem to impress most voters. They are looking only at the bottom line.

It doesn't seem to matter to the fans at Michigan Stadium. Whoever shows up, they pack the place. The last time there was a crowd of less than 100,000 was on October 25, 1975, against Indiana. Michigan had expanded its seating capacity to six figures in 1956, but in the next nineteen years it reached that total just eighteen times—only three in games that did not involve either Michigan State or Ohio State. Into the early '70s, you could always drive to Ann Arbor on the spur of the moment on a Saturday and buy tickets. But the combination of Don Canham's marketing abilities and Schembechler's coaching skill ended all that. Even with 109,000 seats to sell, Michigan is one of football's hottest tickets. Well-heeled alumni cheerfully contribute large sums to the athletic program to guarantee seats between the 20s. Many of Michigan's most avid fans, in fact, never spent a single hour in a classroom there. As Notre Dame used to have its subway alumni, Michigan has its freeway alumni: fans from across the state who strongly identify with its success, who buy the maize-and-blue gear and get all emotional belting out every chorus of "The Victors."

Even an unfamiliar opponent with an unpromising record brings Michigan Stadium an automatic sellout, as it did with Baylor, a considerably less formidable matchup than Colorado.

First-year head coach Dave Roberts said after watching the films of the Colorado game, "First I threw up, and then I cried. They just beat Colorado up and Colorado has some great athletes."

His concerns were well-founded. While Baylor, surprisingly, took its opening drive close enough for a field goal, the first lead on Michigan in 1997, the Wolverines stormed back with five straight touchdowns and a field goal. This time they unleashed the ground attack, with freshman tailback Anthony Thomas and senior Chris Howard each gaining more than a hundred yards.

More significantly, Michigan unleashed Charles Woodson. The junior cornerback lined up on offense and caught a 10-yard touchdown pass from Brian Griese in the first quarter on his first play. He had another 29-yard scoring strike called back on a penalty. He also returned four punts, besides making three unassisted tackles for losses.

"He's awesome," said Roberts. "I don't know how you can prepare to handle him. We tried. He may be the best football player in the country."

When Woodson came on the field, Michigan's offense seemed to attain another level. Designed for safety, it suddenly became a dangerous, unpredictable force. Woodson infused it with energy. He could strike from any direction. Even though his entrance was an obvious signal that Michigan would go to him, defenses seemed incapable of containing him.

"You get the ball to him, it allows for something to happen," said offensive coordinator Mike DeBord.

At this point no one really believed all this would be validated with the Heisman Trophy. The award had all but been conceded to Tennessee quarterback Peyton Manning, whose return to play his senior year at Knoxville was being treated as a triumphal procession to an inevitable Heisman. Only at Michigan and a few other venues in the Midwest did anyone understand that Woodson was something extraordinary, that he could break open a game from either side of the ball and anywhere on the field.

He had come to Ann Arbor from Ross High in Fremont, Ohio. This was President Rutherford B. Hayes' hometown, just east of Toledo, in an area where loyalties are divided between Michigan and Ohio State. One of Moeller's last prize recruits, Woodson had left Fremont as the most sought-after individual since Hayes. He set records in interceptions and rushing. Defensive coordinator Jim Herrmann recalls making the first contact with him.

"I walked into the Fremont gym, saw him take off from the foul line and dunk the basketball," Herrmann says. "I knew right away he was something. But not until I started coaching him did I really understand. Charles is the most competitive person I've ever been around."

Tailback Chris Howard remembers his apprehension when Woodson showed up on the practice field as a freshman in 1995. "I knew all about his rushing records in Ohio and I didn't know where he and I would fit in together on the offense," says Howard, who was then a sophomore. "Then he lined up with the defense and I was like 'What is he doing?' Then I watched him play and there was no doubt in my mind that he would be the best defensive back ever."

Griese noted, however, that initially Woodson was having problems backpedaling. So he called a fade move with receiver Tai Streets in an informal practice and watched Woodson get left five yards behind.

"But by the end of the first week he was giving Tai fits," recalls Griese. "Charles caught on in a hurry. You could see he was a great player. I just had to give him a little introduction to Michigan football."

Woodson spent his first season at Michigan strictly on defense. He was good enough to be voted Big 10 Freshman of the Year. But, in truth, he was bored. He asked Lloyd Carr about the possibility of getting into the offense, too. "He even asked if he could so some punting," says Carr. "He just wanted to be in on as many plays as possible."

In the 1996 season opener against Illinois, Woodson was inserted at running back and broke off a 57-yard ramble. By the third game, against UCLA, pass patterns had been devised for him. He ran for his first offensive touchdown against Indiana, a 48-yard spurt, and caught his first touchdown pass on Michigan State—while making seven tackles in the game. At the end of the season he led the team in interceptions, was third high in rushing, and fifth in receiving.

"I feel whenever I have the ball in my hands something good is going to happen," he said. "I can turn it into 15, 20, whatever yards I need to get into the end zone. I feel I can play cornerback or offense equally. That's my mind-set. I don't want to choose which position is better. I just like being on the field as much as I can."

Woodson needed all the competitiveness in his makeup to overcome his Forrest Gump-like beginnings. He wore leg braces until he was four and was raised by a single mother. Georgia Woodson would come home from her factory job as a forklift operator and from her second job as a waitress and worry how to keep her family of three children together and focused.

Her answer was once-a-week talk and dream sessions held on the living room floor of their apartment.

"Radio off. TV off," she says. "We'd all just sit in a circle and talk. About our plans. About our dreams. About what we'd do if we had money.

"Charles was always going to be a football player. He'd wad up this old sock, throw it into the air, and make believe he was catching it for a touchdown pass while he dived into the sofa. I always told him that he could be whatever he wanted to be. I told him that because my own faith is strong. We are believing people."

"It all goes back to Georgia," says Bob Knapp, the assistant athletic director at Ross High. "If you look for the one thing that influenced the way Charles turned out it has to be her. She was a true matriarch.

"I guess they were ahead of their times. Isn't that what all the self-help books tell you to do—turn off the television and talk to each other? Well, she didn't need any book to figure that out."

Woodson's older sister, Shannon, received a degree from the University of Arkansas while his brother, Terry, graduated from Miami of Ohio.

"Charles never had any doubts that he would be successful," said his closest friend on the Michigan team, Marcus Ray. "I think what his mom did was give him the confidence to go out and accomplish anything he put his mind to. Competitive? You should see him play 'Jeopardy.' Every evening at 7:30 we'd turn on the TV at our place and we'd go at it. And every time he'd beat me, he'd gloat about it, too."

"People see him as arrogant," says Knapp. "I see him as shy. Sometimes during the season I'm sure he wished that all the attention would just go away."

But it was only beginning.

CHAPTER 8

Starting Over

Carr had promised at his introductory press conference that "Michigan will be back." But promises are easy. Now he had to do it.

Significantly, one of the first things he did was drop his role as defensive coordinator. Moeller could never bring himself to step down as offensive coordinator. He was not capable of delegating that kind of authority. In his scheme of things, this was the coach's responsibility. He had to retain that control. Carr, however, felt that continuing to concentrate on defense would mean "turning your back on the field" when Michigan had the ball. "You can't do that and still be on top of your feel and tempo for the game," he said.

That was a big switch and an indicator of the change in outlook at the top.

In a cruel coincidence, however, Michigan had committed to

the earliest start in its history. The 1995 season would open with the Pigskin Classic on August 26, just three months after Carr got the job. The usual preparation time would be shortened by about two weeks. Moreover, the opponent would be Virginia, one of the tougher teams from the Atlantic Coast Conference, coached by one of the game's top tacticians, George Welsh.

The cupboard was not exactly bare. It never is at Michigan. But Carr would enter the season with almost no experience at quarterback. The porous defense of 1994 was a major concern. But he had some cards to play, too.

"I'm not afraid of the pressure," he said, just before the opener. "I know what we have here. Tradition is a tremendous asset for this program, something that can sustain you in time of need. It's very easy to talk about tradition, but after a while it loses its meaning. One thing I'm trying to do is bring that tradition to life.

"But football is not life and death. What I am going to do, with all the strength I have, is keep this team together and let them have fun."

Early in August, Carr assembled his football team, and as night fell he led them onto the floor of Michigan Stadium. He asked them to stand there in the darkness and to think of all the players who had been on that field and all the people who had watched them. He asked his players, his kids, to look around at where they were and think about what it meant. Those who were there said that there was utter silence for nearly fifteen minutes as the young men were left to their own thoughts. The full impact of this place and the connection it gave them with the past rolled over them. If not quite on a par with Napoleon exhorting his army in the shadow of the Pyramids that "Three thousand years of history looks down on you," it was still effective.

With redshirt freshman Scott Dreisbach starting his first game, Michigan trailed 17-0. They came back to beat Virginia on a last-second pass to Mercury Hayes in the back corner of the end zone. Final score, 18-17. The Carr era had begun in memorable fashion.

The euphoria continued for five games. Michigan won them all for the first time in nine years. The media was clamoring for the university to drop the "interim" label and give Carr the job permanently. Players talked about bypassing their senior seasons if Carr did not return. Center Rod Payne said he would "run through brick walls" for him, and credited Carr with giving his players "a fathering experience, something we didn't have with Coach Moeller." Linebacker Jarrett Irons said that "you never saw him stressed out and upset," with the clear implication that had not been the case in preceding seasons.

It seemed like a kinder, gentler face had come to Michigan, and it was one that knew how to win, too.

Then came the bumps. In game six, Northwestern rushed into Michigan Stadium and beat the Wolverines for the first time in thirty years. The Wildcats were the top football story in America, a true Cinderella team. The longtime doormat of the conference was suddenly a power. How strange was that? Only the most dour of Old Blues begrudged them their moment. Still, it went down as Carr's first loss in a big game.

When Tony Banks led Michigan State on a wild comeback at East Lansing and dropped Michigan in the last 84 seconds, loss number two was racked up. That took Michigan out of Rose Bowl contention for the third straight year. Still, a win over Purdue brought Michigan to 8-2, and on November 13 Carr was rewarded with a contract as head coach. Terms were not disclosed. But Michigan had a tradition of one-year contracts and Roberson did not indicate this one was different.

"I don't have any doubts I can do this," said Carr in response. "But I know it won't be easy."

That turned out to be prophetic. Michigan was promptly trampled at Penn State, 27-17. Even a closing win over Ohio State (universally acclaimed because it sent everyone's favorite, Northwestern, to the Rose Bowl) couldn't fully remove the sting of a season that had almost gone right, but not quite. When a lackluster Alamo Bowl showing resulted in another defeat, Michigan was stuck on four losses for the third straight year.

Things did not improve in 1996. This time Carr was in control from the outset, and once more Michigan rolled to a fast 4-0 start. But again the Northwestern game got away. Michigan led 16-0 in the fourth quarter, but a series of breakdowns and mistakes on offense allowed the Wildcats into the game. Accepting the free pass, Northwestern kicked a field goal to win 17-16 in the last 17 seconds. While one loss to Northwestern could be considered as mildly humorous, there was nothing remotely funny about this one. It was almost the 1994 Colorado debacle revisited.

Still, when Carr managed to get his first notch against Michigan State, a 45-29 blowout, the team was 7-1 and poised to make another run at Pasadena. Then, for the second straight year, the wheels came off in November. Traveling to West Lafayette, Indiana, against a thoroughly uninspired Purdue team, Michigan stumbled all over itself. It could not move consistently and blew its best touchdown chance when defensive lineman William Carr was put into the game to carry the ball on a goal line situation and fumbled at the 2. This was really too much. Not only had Michigan committed five turnovers, lost to an inferior team, and been knocked out of Rose Bowl contention again, Carr was diddling around with trick plays on the goal line. Once again the ominous phrase was heard: This isn't how it's done at Michigan.

Moreover, Dreisbach, who had started out with such promise, was fading fast. He threw two interceptions at Purdue and was picked off three more times the following week by Penn State. His thumb, injured in the MSU game, wasn't healing properly. But the young quarterback would not tell the coaches how much pain he was in. The Nittany Lions pounded Michigan, 29-17, the most decisive loss of Carr's tenure. It was the third straight time Michigan had been beaten by Penn State.

It seemed the team was right back where it was when Schembechler arrived in 1969. It could no longer be considered dominant in the Big 10. Penn State had assumed that role and Ohio State was right behind. Since Michigan's last trip to the Rose Bowl, even Wisconsin and Northwestern had gone to Pasadena. The world had turned upside down.

The superb effort at Columbus, with Griese coming off the bench to throw his touchdown pass to Tai Streets, stopped the bleeding. It also blunted Ohio State's drive to a championship for the second straight year. But with the bowl loss to Alabama it was just another 8-4 season. Those who had cheered when Carr was given the job permanently in 1995 (with, as it turned out, a four-year contract) now wondered loudly whether Michigan had acted hastily.

The distemper that had brought down Moeller was working its way through the media and alumni system. This time Carr was the target. Unlike Moeller, however, he seemed able to analyze the criticism and frustration, and figure out a way to deal with it.

"They say that losing has a misery of its own quality," he said in a season-ending interview that seemed to implicitly refer to Moeller's experience two years before. "That's absolutely true. When the expectations are as great as they are, the margin of error is very small. When you expend as much as we all do—

emotionally and physically and mentally—and you fail, the best word, the most descriptive word, is misery.

"But you have to be able to go on. You have to be able to pick yourself off the floor. You can't be distracted by all the critics. I've seen people that in one way or another quit. It can be devastating and paralyzing. There is a part of you that wants to quit. It's the toughest part of the job, there's no question about that.

"The critical part is to be able to separate honest, intelligent criticism from all of the other stuff. If you can't do that, it can get to you. It can get to even the most disciplined guy. It gets to a point where I'm sure it isn't worth it."

Carr gave his team credit for coming up with a remarkable effort against Ohio State. "That revealed character," he said. "There are a lot of young guys on this team who had a chance to play, and they can take this experience into next season. The things you're always concerned about are leadership and attitude. I believe the 1997 team will have these things."

Still, for two straight years, Michigan had stumbled and fallen in the big games, when the title was right on the line. What reason was there to expect anything more from '97?

CHAPTER 9

Lofty Standards

If you believe in college rankings, two grab everyone's attention: the Associated Press football poll and the *U.S. News and World Report* academic ratings. Coaches scoff at the first and college presidents sneer at the latter. But they also react to them. The numbers mean something to the public. When Tufts University, long a small, prestigious, Boston-area private school, crashed the academic Top 25 for the first time in 1996, admissions applications soared. Tufts is now one of the hottest schools in the East.

Only two universities have remained consistently on both lists—Michigan and Notre Dame. Occasionally, a UCLA or North Carolina, a Virginia or Stanford will break into the football rankings. But they find it almost impossible to sustain such success. Only Michigan and Notre Dame, the two top Division I-A football schools in all-time victories, have found the dual formula. But it comes at a cost.

Notre Dame has topped the AP poll seven times since its inception in 1936, more than any other university. But only once in the last twenty years have the Irish finished on top, while Michigan had gone forty-nine years without a title, before the 1997 season. The balance had swung to schools where admission standards were less rigorous. In fact, it seemed only swallowing and breathing were required at some of them. Programs like Miami (Florida) almost seemed to relish a thug-like reputation, while grabbing four national championships between 1983 and 1991. Nebraska also was noted for the high degree of tolerance it afforded misbehaving athletes.

Which is not to say the rules aren't bent at Michigan and Notre Dame. The grades and test scores required for most applicants to these schools are lowered severely for many athletes.

Some believe athletic success feeds into academics, that many outstanding students, especially from the eastern states, will choose a campus such as Michigan for its big-time sports programs. Michigan does have a substantial presence in the East. It draws many students from the New York City area. Walk into Jordon Marsh or Filene's, in Boston, and the most favorably displayed collegiate apparel will bear the names of Boston College, Notre Dame, and Michigan. But Michigan's president, Lee Bollinger, has his doubts about how strong that appeal is.

"It may certainly be a factor," he says. "But I have seen no evidence that it is the decisive factor. In fact, the opposite may be true. We may attract some of our better athletes because they want our academics.

"Of course, our athletic traditions are something we strive to maintain. After I was named to this job I had to fly out to California. I picked up a copy of *Sports Illustrated*—a publication I don't ordinarily read—on the flight. It ranked the Michigan football team eighteenth for the 1997 season and said its long tradition of ascendancy was coming to an end. It was now embarked along the slippery slope to mediocrity.

"I remember thinking to myself how unfortunate it was that I would have to preside over such a sad event. But I would have been much more concerned if someone had told me that Michigan was in imminent danger of falling from the ranks of the top eight or ten great research institutions in America. That would be a matter of grave concern.

"Of course, the exposure you get on national television and in a bowl game—none of that hurts. I know the popular wisdom is that athletic success makes it that much easier to raise funds among alumni. But at the end of the day, they will tell you that it was the total campus experience that created this almost mystical bond they still feel for Ann Arbor. Athletics played a part in that, of course. But not the only part and not the greatest part. That's what we have to keep in perspective."

Still, the blend of athletic and academic excellence is very much a part of the traditions of both schools. And it is a tradition that makes it just that much harder to compete.

"When you recruit for Michigan you have to be a pretty good judge of character," says Schembechler. "I thought that I was. We were looking for the special kids, the ones who can understand the traditions and know their place in it. I took nothing for granted when I was talking to those kids. I noticed the way he spoke to his mom and dad. I talked to his principals and coaches. I gambled a few times and took a few guys I wasn't quite sure about. Usually they eliminated themselves. They couldn't take the discipline. They'd quit or get into trouble. I'd try to let the seniors handle it, but if they couldn't, the guy had to go. It's too disruptive to keep a guy like that around. No matter how good he is, that isn't the way it can be here."

"To be a Michigan man," said the team's co-captain Eric

Mayes, of Kalamazoo, before the 1997 Notre Dame game, "you have to know the tradition of Michigan. That's why you come here. You come here to wear those funny helmets. You come here because they're the winningest program in college football. You come here because they play in front of 100,000 fans week in and week out.

"You come here because they have legends like Bo Schembechler who walk up and down Schembechler Hall. Michigan is tradition and you want to be a part of it. Every man on this team will tell you who played in the first Rose Bowl. They'll tell you the last time Michigan won the national championship. They'll tell you the tradition of Michigan because that's what Michigan is and you want to continue that tradition."

And when Michigan plays Notre Dame, the two greatest traditions in the game collide.

"That's one of the reasons I don't think we should be playing them," says Schembechler. "When you're Michigan, you're the biggest game on every other team's schedule. Everyone is looking for you. We're the top game for Michigan State. The top game for Ohio State. When we play Notre Dame we're the top game on their schedule, even though they may not want to admit it. When Penn State joined the Big 10 and came on our schedule, Notre Dame should have gone off. That's just too many tough games. You lose focus on the Big 10 race."

Ohio State's John Cooper went so far as to propose a Big 10 freeze on games with Notre Dame, unless the Irish agree to join the conference and make it a Big 12.

Michigan and Notre Dame had not met for thirty-five years when the series was revived in 1978. In thirteen of the next fifteen games played, both teams were ranked in the top twenty on game day. Ten of those games were decided by a touchdown or less.

Moreover, five times Michigan had gone in with the higher ranking and lost. This was shaping up as another of those times.

Notre Dame was angry and dangerous. It had been beaten badly by Purdue and Michigan State and under its first-year coach, Bob Davies, was in danger of losing three straight for the first time in more than thirty years. The Irish were calling on their deep tradition for the major effort that could salvage their season. Michigan was a two-touchdown favorite. But for the first time in this young season it was going to look fear in the face and be tested.

CHAPTER 10

Broom at the Top

There were supposed to be no shocks at Michigan. That was part of the tradition. Decade after decade, the stability of the program was the wonder of college football. From 1921, when Fielding Yost was appointed athletic director, to 1988, when Don Canham stepped down, only three men held the office. Those two and Fritz Crisler. Three men in sixty-seven years. But Canham's retirement set in motion a chain of events that eventually would rock the program to its foundation.

It started when Schembechler decided he wanted the job. He had worked well with Canham and didn't like the idea of starting over again with someone new. Moreover, by 1988 he knew his coaching time was running out. He had undergone bypass surgery the previous year, although he angrily waved off any suggestion that his health was an issue. But he did want to be absolutely sure he would have a free hand in naming his successor when the time came. He wanted it to be Moeller, but a new AD with ideas of his own might mess that up.

Canham's retirement coincided with a period of transition at the top of the university. Former president Robben Fleming had been called out of retirement to serve as interim executive after the surprise resignation of Harold Shapiro. So there was no strong force as a countervailing weight against Schlembecher's push. Fleming and the Board of Regents wanted Bo to step down as coach if he took the AD job. Canham also suggested it might be better if Schembechler "delegated authority." But Bo had no intention of stepping down from the job he loved before he was good and ready. Crisler, after all, had held both positions for seven years. It was difficult to say no to Bo. You'd need someone without an interim in front of his title to do that. In the end, Fleming and the Regents agreed. In April 1988, at the start of his twentieth year at Michigan, Schembechler was named athletic director.

Whatever reservations Canham had about the move he kept to himself, because he knew some alternatives were far worse. Yost had established the precedent that kept the athletic department semi-independent. Although his relationship with the university's presidents was cordial and the final word always rested with them, Yost saw to it that they remained at a distance. That gave him control of department finances, a power that he handed down to Crisler and Canham. But Canham understood that independence would only last as long as a strong personality occupied the AD's chair. Bo was nothing if not a strong personality.

The news stories marking Schembechler's appointment also noted that Jack Weidenbach had been named senior associate athletic director. As it turned out, this was the real story.

Weidenbach did not come out of athletics or business. He was, instead, an inside man at the university, the director of business operations. He was a professional administrator who knew where all the money trails led and had a long association with the rest of the university community. "I know all the deans of all seventeen schools and colleges," he liked to say. He had also known the university's newly appointed president, James J. Duderstadt, from the time he had joined the faculty.

So Schembechler was able to continue doing what he enjoyed most without worrying about the minutiae of administration. Weidenbach handled that. And twenty months later, just before the 1990 Rose Bowl, when Schembechler felt it was time, he announced he would step down as coach and turn the job over to Moeller.

"It's time to go," he said. "Who could ask for a greater career than I've had? It's not that I've done everything in football, but I have coached Michigan."

What no one foresaw was just three weeks later, he also would resign as AD to accept the job of president of the Detroit Tigers. Duderstadt immediately moved to have Weidenbach named as Schembechler's successor, answerable directly to the president. That is exactly what Canham had feared would happen. Duderstadt was going to take hands-on control of the athletic program.

"It didn't change until Bo left, and then it changed almost overnight," says Canham. "You have to have an athletic background first or you don't know what's going on. You just don't know what to look for. When I was hiring a football coach I knew exactly what I wanted and knew Bo was it in the first fifteen minutes of our interview. What would Duderstadt know about that?"

"Don Canham may not like it," Duderstadt responded, "but

this is the new nature of intercollegiate athletics. There was a sense that independent athletic departments had drifted too far away from the educational values of the university. Under the NCAA rules, college presidents are now the ultimate authority, and in the end the blame will wind up on the president's desk."

Said Canham: "The problem is Duderstadt confused presidential control for presidential management."

Weidenbach was sixty-five years old when he got the job and it was understood this would be a short-term appointment. But it gave Duderstadt the chance to consolidate his control, and in four years he named another close associate, Joe Roberson, to the job.

Roberson was an experienced fund-raiser, leading the $1 billion Campaign for Michigan, and had served in a variety of inside jobs at Michigan since 1966. He was fifty-eight and his appointment was expected to restore continuity to the department. But few in the media saw Roberson as ready for prime time, saying he was unused to the high pressure of major college athletics. At an institution where there weren't supposed to be any shocks, Roberson was confronted with one after another. His responses seemed inconsistent, unsure, confused.

He was accused of a rush to judgment in the Moeller incident, giving the coach an ultimatum to accept disciplinary action before an investigation had been completed. He said Moeller had resigned and then had to backtrack when it was revealed Moeller had been paid $400,000 to leave. On the other hand, he let the situation in the basketball program fester, failing to move decisively as evidence of misfeasance and lack of control in Steve Fisher's program mounted.

Roberson seemed overmatched and the athletic programs were adrift. When Duderstadt resigned and was replaced by Lee

Bollinger in 1997, it was evident that Roberson would soon be out as well. It also was clear that Bollinger believed in backing off and letting the AD run the department.

"There are four things a university president should be concerned about in regard to athletics," says Bollinger. "He should help define it and respect its place as a critical element in the academic community, as much as dance and poetry. He should shape its general values. For example, I did not for a minute think that our basketball program had violated NCAA standards. My concern was that it had violated our standards.

"He must make the rules clear; that we will not tolerate a policy of two or three mistakes. And he must make sure the people he appoints are capable of implementing and refining these policies."

One week before the 1997 football season began, Bollinger named Tom Goss as the new AD. A successful businessman, a former Michigan football player (on the last team before Schembechler arrived), his appointment seemed to symbolize a return to the model that had worked before. More important, Bollinger seemed inclined to go back to granting limited autonomy—overseeing the department instead of managing it. Within a few weeks, Goss had fired Fisher and had spoken out clearly against the policy of selling season football tickets before all students had been given a chance to buy them.

As much as anything else that happened in 1997, the arrival of Goss seemed to indicate Michigan was back on track.

CHAPTER 11

Family Ties
September 27. Michigan 21, Notre Dame 14

If Notre Dame was only a shadow of its former self, the Irish were giving no evidence of it at Michigan Stadium. Instead, they had nullified the Michigan defense that had destroyed two previous opponents.

The Irish ran up 227 yards of offense in the first half, controlling the ball on two long drives. Each took more than 10 minutes and ended in touchdowns. The second went 98 yards, and ended with 18 seconds left in the half.

Senior quarterback Ron Powlus executed beautifully behind strong pass blocking, and Notre Dame's mix of plays seemed to catch Michigan consistently off-balance. The half ended with Michigan behind, 14-7.

In other seasons, the big crowd would have been sulking uneasily or sitting in silence. But when Michigan came on the field to start the second half, the huge throng came to its feet and began to cheer wildly for the Wolverines. Co-captain Jon Jensen heard it and a thrill went through him.

"To feel that kind of energy in the stadium," he says. "I'd never felt it like that before. It was like they were going to will us back into this game. We were down and they were cheering like crazy. That's when I knew this year was going to be different. There was just something there that I had never felt before.

"We got into the huddle after the kickoff and Brian [Griese] was so calm. Here was this noise crashing down all around us, and it was like he was just this tower of calm. Every one of us knew then that he could get it done."

In a play that was almost a rerun of the pass that beat Ohio State the previous year, Griese hit Streets on a slant across the middle. The receiver sprinted into the end zone from 41 yards out. Tie game, 14-14. Now the crowd was screaming.

Carr looked around, as if to reassure himself that yes, this was actually Michigan Stadium, home of the diffident. After the season ended, he listed this play as one of the three biggest of the year on offense.

Now the Michigan defense roared to life and forced Notre Dame to punt from its own 8. It took just seven plays for the Wolverines to drive down the field for the 21-14 lead, with Chris Floyd barging in from 14 yards.

The scoring was over, but no one knew that yet. For the next quarter and a half this game would go on a ride that had the entire stadium hanging on.

After scoring twice, the Michigan attack went back in its shell. Worse yet, it started coughing up the ball. A Michigan fumble started the fourth quarter and Notre Dame drove to the 4. A delay-of-game penalty pushed them back to the 9. On the next play Powlus, scrambling under pressure, was intercepted by defensive back Tommy Hendricks in the end zone.

Then Russell Shaw fumbled a Griese pass and Notre Dame took over again at the Michigan 42. This time they couldn't move the ball and had to punt. Floyd fumbled a handoff and Notre Dame began to move again. But on fourth and two at the 19, Autry Denson was crushed by Sam Sword and Rob Renes. Michigan ran out the last three minutes of the game.

As the clock ticked down, Carr paced along the sidelines, thrusting his fist into the air.

"I had no idea I was doing that," he said later. "But those fourth-quarter stands were so unimaginably big. That was a very emotional game. I was so happy to come out of there with the win."

"I still believe that the Hendricks interception was our season," says Jim Herrmann. "At that point, it could have gone either way. But you measure a season in plays like that. The funny thing is, Powlus could have run it in. The lane was clear for him."

"That was a win and that's all it was," said Griese. "But I'm glad we finally got into a game that went down to the fourth quarter. You find something out about your team."

The best thing about the game, however, was what Michigan found out about its quarterback. Any doubts about Griese's ability to perform under pressure, to bring the team back, were dispelled.

"I'd come so close to leaving," he said. "I had my degree and I had made up my mind to start graduate school. But it was something my older brother, Jeff, told me. 'You know, when you leave school you'll be working for a very long time.' I thought about that and it made sense. So I came back."

It is hard to imagine how the season would have gone if he hadn't.

Brian was too young to remember his father's glory days with the Dolphins, but old enough to know the pain of losing a mother to cancer. Judy Griese died in 1988 when her youngest son was thirteen and his two older brothers had already left for college. It was just Brian and his father in the house in Coral Gables. They sat across from each other at the breakfast table every morning, attended school functions together, drove to games. The elder Griese, everybody's All American, was suddenly alone at forty-three, without a companion. Brian became his buddy.

Bob already was established as a television analyst, teaming up with veteran play-by-play man Keith Jackson on Saturday games. Sometimes Brian would accompany his dad on these trips, having dinner with him and Jackson on the night before the game.

He also was growing up. At 6-3 and more than 200 pounds, he was bigger than his dad and two brothers and had developed into an outstanding quarterback at Miami's Columbus High, setting career records for passing. He also had turned into a great golfer and tennis player.

"Brian's strength, his intelligence, decision-making, and the way he approaches the game are similar to mine," says his father. "He also makes few turnovers and has the leadership, which is a lot like the way I played. I scrambled better and was quicker," says the elder Griese with a small smile, "though he won't agree with that."

"The bottom line is they both knew how to win," says Michigan quarterbacks coach Stan Parrish. "They both have the reputation of being cerebral guys. But the one thing I sensed about Brian is his sense of calm. Calmness is the best attribute a quarterback can possess."

On one notable occasion, the calm deserted him. After losing the starting job to Dreisbach in 1995, the frustration that Griese tried to bottle up came welling out. One night he had a little too much to drink and threw a chair through the window of an Ann Arbor bar. He was mortified and contrite. And Carr understood.

"With all of us, we make mistakes when we're young," says Carr. "The question is, what do you learn from your mistakes? Brian learned a great deal from his. What he really learned was respect. He came back to the team and accepted his role. He didn't mope around and become a distraction. He showed up every day with enthusiasm and determination. How could I not respect that as a coach?"

"I came to understand that when it comes to the spotlight, it didn't really make any difference that I was Bob Griese's son," says Brian. "When you play quarterback for Michigan, the spotlight is on you. You can't control the brightness. You can only control yourself."

Brian's career at Michigan led to some deep chin-stroking at the offices of the American Broadcasting Company, his father's employer. Not wanting to appear partial, ABC would not permit the father to cover any of his son's games in 1995. Bob was annoyed but accepted the decision. But with Brian relegated to a backup role in 1996, the network relented. Besides, someone recalled how former race car driver Ned Jarrett had covered his son Dale's win at the 1993 Daytona 500. It resulted in honest emotion and emotion made good TV. Finally, in the Ohio State game, the situation everyone had been waiting for arrived. Brian Griese came into the game as a replacement and led the Wolverines to an upset win.

Bob coolly referred to his son as "Griese" throughout the game. "At one point," he told *Sports Illustrated*, "I remember saying that Ohio State better get after the quarterback, send in some blitzers, confuse him. I watched the tape of the game later and thought to myself, 'I'm telling them to attack my son. I can't believe it.'"

Griese's longtime partner, Jackson, who had known Brian since he was a child, ended the telecast by saying, "I guess there are going to be some good stories to tell around the dinner table at the Griese household this Christmas."

Going into 1997 there was no question that ABC would continue to assign Griese to Michigan games. It turned out to be a story that caught the country's imagination. Fans were willing to overlook any possible conflict of interest. Magazines and newspapers ran several feature stories.

More important, father and son were able to share the season. On New Year's Day, they brought the entire nation to tears as their inter-generational family story reached its conclusion.

But as the Grieses wrapped up their respective details on the Notre Dame game, that was still well in the future.

CHAPTER 12

October 4. Michigan 37, Indiana 0

Even the easy games look hard this season. Indiana, ordinarily, is barely a blip on Michigan's schedule, as far as football is concerned. Basketball was something else again, and for years Schembechler and Bobby Knight formed a mutual admiration coaching society. Each recognized in the other a kindred spirit. But Indiana remained first, last, and always a basketball school, to which the period from September to November was an empty quarter.

Its former head coach, Bill Mallory, had been a Michigan assistant under Schembechler. Mallory's son, Mike, even started for Bo at linebacker for three seasons in the mid-'80s, while his father coached the Hoosiers. The elder Mallory gave it his best, took Indiana to six bowl games, and won more games than any other coach in school history. But only once (1987) did he come close to a Big 10 title. The talent just did not come his way. The imprint of basketball was simply too strong.

Michigan had beaten Indiana twenty-two of the last twenty-three times the schools had met. Going back to 1900, Indiana had won only nine games. This time it was different, though. Indiana again had turned to a former Michigan assistant for a head coach. Cam Cameron was regarded as a brilliant innovator on offense. He had been with the Washington Redskins for the previous three seasons and his name was mentioned frequently for NFL head coaching vacancies.

Cameron was determined to change the old order in Bloomington. He had gone on a statewide bus tour with some of his players to raise enthusiasm and stimulate future recruiting. He joked that his preseason camp had "looked like a day care center. The coaches were almost as young as the players." He even changed the Hoosiers' helmet insignia to resemble that of the five-time Super Bowl champions, the San Francisco 49ers. He saw his job as creating a tradition that could stand with Michigan's. Some at Michigan made no secret that they would have preferred the thirty-six-year-old Cameron to the fifty-two-year-old Carr.

So there was that connection. The conference opener also happened to be Indiana's homecoming, the most emotional game on any team's schedule. Cameron shrugged that this was merely a coincidence. Indiana's homecoming always fell on the same weekend and the schedules were made by the neutral Big 10 computer in Chicago. This also would be the first road game after three adoring sessions in front of Michigan's newly enthused fans in Ann Arbor. That all seemed enough to be wary about.

As it turned out, Carr could have saved his worry beads.

"Some people might have tried to score 100 but Lloyd didn't," said Cameron after the annihilation. "I told him that I was grateful for that." It was 31-0 at the half and the Wolverines were content to let the rest of the time go by with just two field goals.

Michigan, instead, took the chance to work out the kinks in its offense. It had appeared uncertain against Notre Dame. The point was to maintain a balance between Griese's passing and the inside running game. The plan worked. Freshman Anthony Thomas ran for 65 yards, Streets caught another touchdown pass, and Griese got to relax for the fourth quarter, with Brady taking the controls. Indiana managed just 157 yards on offense. It was pretty much your standard Michigan-Indiana game.

This one had a melancholy note, however. Co-captain Eric Mayes, a senior linebacker who had spoken so movingly of Michigan's tradition the week before, went down in the first quarter with career-ending knee ligament damage.

In its own way, Mayes' story was just as moving as Griese's. Undersized at 220 pounds and not especially fast, he had come out of the Kalamazoo suburb of Portage, where he captained the football and basketball teams at Northern High. Ignored by the major schools, he accepted a scholarship from Xavier of New Orleans. But he left after one season and decided to take his chances at Michigan as a walk-on. His headlong style on special teams in 1996 brought him the co-captaincy and the starter's role at inside linebacker.

Dhani Jones was watching from the sidelines as Mayes went down; his heart sank.

"I remember thinking, 'God forbid, it's anything serious,'" Jones says. "And then 'Eric, you better get up.' And that's about the only thing that there was time for. The next minute I was in the game. The hunt was on and I was the prey.

"I had started games before. Your name is listed and they call it out. You dig your claws in the hardest and you're the man. And I always knew that when this moment came that I had to be ready.

But to see Eric coming out like that, the suddenness of it...my goodness. I looked up in the stands where I knew my mom and dad were sitting. I can always spot her because she's always wearing this big, huge yellow—pardon me, maize—hat. I saw 'em there and that was my motivation. Time to do it. Of course, it helped that my sister goes to Indiana. That was kind of a motivation, too."

Dhani Makalani Jones is his full name. The middle name is Hawaiian, a state he is especially fond of. The first name is East Indian and means, says Jones, "thinking man."

"I didn't have any name for about a week," he says. "My parents decided to wait and see if I would take on a name of my own. I guess they liked Dhani, too, because that's what George Harrison, the Beatle, called his son."

Jones' mother is a medical doctor. His father retired from the Army. He has traveled extensively ("the best was the safari in Kenya when lions came right up to the front door"). He plans to go into medicine, maybe surgery. He showed up for this interview wearing a Curious George tee shirt and carrying an organic chemistry textbook.

"My parents were very big on inspirational sayings," says Jones. "'Inch by inch everything's a cinch' was one of them. And '*Do Good* is not a noun.' Maybe it sounds a little corny but I've always responded to things like that. That's probably the reason I wound up at Michigan.

"I grew up right outside Washington, D.C., in Potomac, Maryland. But they showed us that M flag sitting up on the Moon [left by astronaut Jim Lovell], and I knew about the academics and the tradition, and I felt this was something for me to attain. You know that sign in the Michigan locker room: 'Those who stay will be champions.' When a person is young those are words to live by. That's the definition of competition. There's nothing better. I love that. Besides, both my mom and dad went here. That factored in, too."

Jones finished the Indiana game with nine tackles, leading the defense. He was not moved out of the starter's position for the rest of the year.

Michigan had now given up a total of 20 points in its four games, not a single one in the fourth quarter. Only Notre Dame has crossed its goal line.

"When I say Michigan defense, I envision eleven winged helmets knocking the hell out of somebody," says Herrmann. "No superstars. Just eleven guys going after the football with reckless abandon."

"Our motto is 'Get the ball back. Do whatever it takes.'"

"Playing that defense is an awakening," says Jones. "You can be free as a team. You can suck energy from each other. All that adrenaline is pumping and you're feeling like 110 percent. Everybody on the same page. I can't describe that feeling.

"I mean I've been going at it full tilt and someone can come off the other line and pancake me and my reaction is 'If you're good enough to get through our defense and do that to me, well, good for you. But you won't do it again.'

"By the end of the season, I was pretty busted up. But I had so much energy, it was like I was drawing it from nature. It was like that book *The Celestine Prophecy*. You become aware of you inner vibrations as a person, the essence of your spiritual power. It is awesome. It was a healing in itself."

When the first AP Poll for October came out, Michigan had moved up to sixth. That matched the highest ranking the Wolverines had attained under Carr. It had been reached one year earlier and then was snatched away by Northwestern.

The next team on the 1997 schedule was Northwestern.

CHAPTER 13

The Loyalists

Each time their younger sister brought a young man home to meet the family, the two Grossman brothers put the poor devil to the test. Richard and David would invite Debbie's unsuspecting suitor to join them in front of a television set and watch a Michigan football game.

"We didn't ask much. It wasn't a quiz or anything. We were just looking for someone who acted as if he knew what was going on," says Richard innocently. "But if his attention wandered or he started asking dumb questions, that was it. We did what we had to do. He never would have made it in this family."

This went on for years, until their sister finally picked the right one. She was married in the spring of 1998 to an attorney who had to be scraped off the ceiling after Michigan won the Rose Bowl. He was a Grossman kind of guy.

Michigan football fans may not be quite as outrageous as those from other schools. They probably do not approach the all-out devotion of those in Nebraska or the quasi-religious fervor that sweeps many of the southern schools. There is, after all, another large university in the same state and professional teams in all four major sports. But in terms of dogged loyalty mixed with sheer numbers, Michigan wins going away.

"It's like an alternate life," says John Husband, who publishes a sports newsletter in Waterford, Michigan. "Logically, I know that it's wrong to put that kind of emotional investment in a bunch of kids who are essentially just teenagers. But it gets in your blood. It's my team and I still get bummed out when they lose.

"I'm getting better, though. It used to take days before I'd get over a bad one. I still remember crying my eyes out as a kid when they went down to Purdue as number one in 1976 and Mike Lantry missed the last-second field goal. I was listening to Bob Ufer on the radio and he just kept saying: 'He missed. He missed. He missed.' So slow and mournful. I didn't even want to eat dinner or talk to anyone for days.

"But I got married last August," says Husband. "She knew what she was getting into. So that brings me out of the funk faster."

On the Thursday night before every Michigan game, Howard Feldman used to paint his garage in the Detroit suburb of Southfield. The design was always an exhortatory message to the team.

"If it was Notre Dame, it would be something like 'Stomp the Irish,'" he explained. "If it was Purdue, it was 'Batter the Boilermakers.' Nothing too fancy. It got to be a thing in the neighborhood, everyone wondering what I was going to put up there each week."

When his children attended Michigan, Feldman bought a house close to the stadium. The stated reason was that it would

Bo Schembechler stepped down after the 1989 season as one of Michigan's most successful and beloved coaches. His singular emphasis on winning the Big Ten, however, was viewed by some as an obstacle to Michigan's chances of winning a national championship. (AP/Wide World Photos)

Michigan's longtime athletic director Don Canham turned UM football into a success off the field as well. (AP/Wide World Photos)

Gary Moeller succeeded Bo as head coach in 1990. For the first time in years, perhaps ever, a UM coach publicly made the national championship a goal. But early success was followed by a string of subpar years that culminated in Moeller's resignation in 1995 after an altercation at a suburban Detroit restaurant. Here's Moeller with Notre Dame coach Lou Holtz in 1990. (AP/Wide World Photos)

Lloyd Carr, longtime assistant under Bo and Moeller, addresses the media at the 1995 press conference naming him Michigan's head coach. As Moeller before him, Carr's first two teams fell short of most expectations. But during those years Carr was quietly laying the foundation for 1997. (AP/Wide World Photos)

Kordell Stewart's hail mary pass on the final play of Colorado's 1994 victory over the Wolverines in Ann Arbor was a gut-wrenching symbol of UM's mid-nineties frustrations. (Allsport)

A preseason question mark, quarterback Brian Griese answered a lot of questions, affirmatively, in Michigan's opening game rout of Colorado, 27-3, which avenged the 1994 heartbreak. Michigan's defense, expected to be solid, performed even better than that. It was a roaring portent. (Allsport)

Wolverines' Sam Sword (93), James Hall (56), and Glen Steele (81) combine forces to bring down a Notre Dame ballcarrier. UM rallied to top the Irish 21-14 in the Wolverines' first real test of the season. (Allsport)

Charles Woodson displayed his multiple talents early in the season. Here, he goes over a Baylor defender to haul in this Griese pass in Michigan's 38-3 workmanlike victory over the Bears. It was the Wolverines' second consecutive convincing victory. (AP/Wide World Photos)

The offensive line, led by
Jon Jansen, took over
the Notre Dame game in
the second half and
never looked back from
there the rest of the
season. (Allsport)

UM's Ian Gold (20), James Whitley (5), and Diallo Johnson (9) swarm to
the ball in Michigan's 37-0 shutout of the Hoosiers. Coached by former UM
assistant Cam Cameron, the Hoosiers struggled all day against UM's hungry
defense, which was beginning to gain attention outside of Ann Arbor and
the Midwest. (Allsport)

(*Left*) Gary Barnett had achieved the unthinkable, leading Northwestern to the 1996 Rose Bowl and defeating the Wolverines in back-to-back years. The 1997 grudge match restored some order to the Big Ten, as Michigan efficiently dispatched the Wildcats 23-6. (AP/Wide World Photos).

(*Right*) Following their biggest scare of the year, a 28-24 nail-biter win against Iowa the week before, the Wolverines ground out a 23-7 victory over intrastate rival Michigan State. Led by linebacker Dhani Jones, the UM defense stifled the Spartans' passing game, leaving little running room for State's only offensive weapon, star running back Sedrick Irvin (33). At 7-0, Michigan had passed its first big test. (AP/Wide World Photos)

Russell Shaw comes down with a pass in Michigan's eighth victory of the season, a 24-3 mauling of Minnesota. More and more it appeared that this UM team would not lose games it should win. (Allsport)

It all came together in Michigan's win over nemesis Penn State, by the improbable score of 34-8. The Wolverines made a loud statement that they were not about to shrink from the national title picture. (*Opposite*) Running backs Chris Howard and Anthony Thomas had big days, and (*above*) the defense continued to impress, causing many, including Bo Schembechler, to suggest that perhaps this was one of college football's greatest defenses ever. (AP/Wide World Photos)

Charles Woodson's big day against hated rival Ohio State may have clinched the Heisman Trophy for him. Here, he returns a punt 78 yards for a touchdown. Although OSU made it close at the end, the Wolverines persevered 20-14 to win the Big Ten and to conclude an undefeated season. (AP/Wide World Photos)

Heisman Trophy winner Charles Woodson shows why, leaping high to inter-
cept this Ryan Leaf pass in the first half of the 1998 Rose Bowl. Pitted as
Michigan's stubborn defense against Washington State's high-octane
offense, the Rose Bowl was a tight game in which both units had their
moments. (AP/Wide World Photos)

Tai Streets sprints for the end zone in the Rose Bowl. While much of the pregame focus was on the UM defense, Streets came up with a big day. (Allsport)

Michigan defensive tackle Josh Williams (91) sacks Ryan Leaf.
(AP/Wide World Photos)

Ryan Leaf is thwarted in his last-ditch attempt to rally his Cougars past UM in the Rose Bowl. Michigan's 21-16 victory in the 84th Rose Bowl capped an undefeated season and earned Michigan the long-coveted title of national champions. (AP/Wide World Photos)

Heisman Trophy winner Charles Woodson strikes the statue's pose
during UM's national championship rally at Crisler Arena in Ann Arbor.
(AP/Wide World Photos)

Charles Woodson poses with the Heisman Trophy after becoming the first primarily defensive player ever to win the award. He is pictured at the Downtown Athletic Club in New York. (AP/Wide World Photos)

be cheaper for his kids to live there than for him to pay rent to someone else. His family suspects the real reason is that it put him even closer to the holy of holies.

More merchandise with the Michigan logo on it is sold annually than that of any other school. According to Collegiate Licensing Co. (CLC), an Atlanta-based firm that leads in the sale of such goods, Michigan and Notre Dame rank first and second—even though before 1997 these were the only schools on CLC's top ten list that had not won a championship in the '90s.

"People usually buy goods from winners," says Bill Battle, president of CLC. "With Michigan it started to build with the Fab Five basketball teams in the early '90s. But football jerseys and tee shirts with the M logo have always been a steady seller for us. Because it's national. Everywhere you go in the country you find Michigan alumni and this is their way of participating. Besides, the colors are pretty cool."

The sports licensing business has grown tenfold since 1984 and now has estimated annual sales of $2.5 billion. In fact, counterfeit logos generate more illegal income than drugs, according to CLC. Michigan's share of the pot is close to $7 million a year.

So Sue Watkins was not terribly surprised when she checked her store by phone on the morning after the Rose Bowl. She owns an outlet of a statewide company called M Let's Go Blue in the Detroit suburb of Royal Oak.

"My store manager told me that the lines were out the front and onto the street," she says. "The stuff was just flying out the doors. Anything that had a national championship emblem on it. Lapel pins, flags, the locker-room baseball caps that the players were wearing on TV.

"How big was it? I'd rather not give out the numbers, but I can tell you it was a major, major impact. We were up to our eyeballs.

January was a wonderful time for my store...and anyone else who handles Michigan merchandise.

"But I can't say that I was surprised. I got into this business eleven years ago because of this phenomenon. Even when Nebraska and the Florida schools were winning all the championships, our business was good. I knew it would go through the roof this time. Look, you've got a school with the greatest number of living alumni, plus twice as many as that who are drawn by success. This was a major payoff for them."

For Larry Seder it was a payoff in which he had invested heavily. Seder graduated from Michigan in 1957 and has owned season tickets since. Most seasons he gets to every game. What makes this remarkable is that Seder lives in Boston, about seven hundred miles from Michigan Stadium.

"It isn't that hard," he insists. "You catch an early morning plane, have breakfast with friends, get to the game, and catch an evening flight back. Many times I'm home in time for dinner.

"But it is getting harder. When every home game started at 1:00 P.M., you could line up your flight reservations months in advance. It wasn't any more demanding than spending the day playing golf. But then they started fooling around with the kickoff times to accommodate TV. Then the airlines began demanding Saturday-night stayovers to get the low fares.

"So it's getting tougher and I'm getting older," says Seder. "But to catch a winner after all those years, and so unexpectedly, it was an experience."

Even Seder has to take a back seat, though, to Jay Deeds, who lives in Grosse Pointe Park. He doesn't have to fly to the games. A one-hour drive out Interstate 94 will do. But the eighty-five-year-old Deeds hasn't missed a game at Michigan Stadium since 1952, and has been to every game, home and away, since 1966. That's 372 in a row.

His home is decorated, floor to ceiling, with Michigan memorabilia. Signed photographs, old ticket stubs, schedules. Moreover, he isn't even an alumnus, and grew up in Ohio.

"I'm very deeply involved in everything I do," he offers by way of explanation. "The whole process of getting to the games has become sort of a game in itself for me."

When Deeds began his streak, Michigan already was three years past its last national championship. So he can say without much fear of contradiction that the 1997 season was the most exciting he had seen. "They played like a team and outsmarted their opponents," he says. "That's what made them fun to watch."

Still, Michigan fans all know their history. That's what was making them nervous as the season advanced into October. The recent history of the Northwestern series was not good. For the last two years, Michigan's hopes for undefeated seasons had been dashed by the Wildcats. And that's who was coming to Ann Arbor.

CHAPTER 14

October 11. Michigan 23, Northwestern 6

When Gary Barnett arrived at Northwestern, one of the first things he did was annoy Michigan. He accused it of cheating. Before the 1992 game, the new football coach said that Gary Moeller's method of sending substitutions into the game at the last possible second, out of a scrum of players milling along the sideline, was not cricket. Moeller was incensed and was still steaming after his team had administered their ritual thrashing of the Wildcats at Evanston.

You just didn't say things like that about Michigan football. There was no surer way to provoke the Wolverines. Who was this Barnett guy anyhow? Didn't he know the Big 10 pecking order? The Northwestern program was a joke. It had set records for futility throughout the '80s. The team once went thirty-four straight games without a win, a record for a Division 1-A School. Not since Ara Parseghian left for Notre Dame after the 1963 season had Northwestern been a serious challenger for the Big 10 title. Michigan had beaten them nineteen straight times since 1965 by an average score of 39-7.

Northwestern was getting beaten by the numbers. It was a small, private school; the only non-public institution in the Big 10. Its admission standards were more rigorous than Michigan's (at least, when it came to in-state admissions). A sample Northwestern joke: What do players who beat the Wildcats call a Northwestern graduate five years after the game? Boss.

But the athletic program had become hopelessly uncompetitive. Media analysts, in fact, were constantly wondering why the Big 10 didn't dump them, let them play teams of their own caliber: Wake Forest and Vanderbilt and Stanford, other academically outstanding schools in high-powered conferences. The problem was, Northwestern couldn't beat them, either.

Barnett understood all this. He knew Northwestern usually lost the Michigan game the day after the schedules were printed. Its players went into the season knowing it was hopeless. So Barnett decided to pick a fight, show his players that one way or another you've got to stand up to the big guys.

Michigan won that 1992 meeting 40-7 and then didn't see Barnett again for two years. Meanwhile, he had loaded up. Using academics as a draw, Barnett had attracted a group of bright, talented athletes. They were maybe a little undersized by Big 10 standards but ready to play a physical game, get in and mix it up with the top teams without backing down.

In 1995, they shocked the Wolverines in Ann Arbor, 19-13, in a tremendous, hard-hitting game. The next year, even with the Wolverines forewarned, Michigan collapsed in the fourth quarter, blowing a 16-0 lead.

Graduation and injuries had thinned out the quality players

Barnett had brought in. They were only off to a 2-4 start and Michigan, once again, was a solid 24-point favorite. But a few nagging doubts persisted.

"This certainly does not want to be known as the Michigan team that lost three straight times to Northwestern," said Carr. That actually had happened once before, but not since the 1930s.

"I don't think of this game in terms of the *R-word*, meaning *Revenge*," said Griese. "I think of it in terms of the *R-word*, meaning *Respect*. We gave away games both years. They had no reason to respect us. You have got to get fired up for this game. They are the two-time defending Big 10 champions, and if that doesn't get you ready you don't have red blood in your body."

Griese may not have been an expert in hematology but he had the right motivational ideas. Michigan rolled over Northwestern in a cold-blooded, methodical execution. If not quite as appalling as some of the poundings it had handed the Wildcats in the previous two decades, it was just as thorough.

Griese had taken it upon himself to make up for his two turnovers he felt had given away the game in 1995. This time he was 23 of 36 passing, with no turnovers. He hit his tight end, Tuman, for a 10-yard touchdown pass, and then repeated on a 2-yard dinker. But it took time to get the offense going. It started slowly, with several offside and motion calls stalling drives in the first half. Michigan was ahead just 13-3 at the break. The game seemed to be falling into the same dangerous pattern as the previous two years.

Except for one thing. The defense was stifling anything Northwestern tried. The Wildcats had a minus 2 yards rushing for the first half, and quarterback Tim Hughes was scrambling all over the field trying to avoid the relentless Michigan rush.

"We came out a little flat," said Woodson. "But when the

offense is having trouble you've just got to get more aggressive on defense. This game has been on our mind for a year. It's been our hump ever since I've been here. Today we were going to get over that hump, no matter what."

It was more than a hump, actually. For the first time in eleven years Michigan was now two games into the Big 10 season undefeated and untied. For all the dominance of the Schembechler years, only twice had Michigan teams been able to run the board in the conference. If not Ohio State at the end, it was always some lesser team, waiting in the weeds, that picked them off. The entire conference schedule was a land mine that could explode if trodden upon unwarily.

Carr had tried to emphasize that to his team early in the going. He compared the schedule Michigan faced to a climb of Mt. Everest. To drive that point home, he brought in a guest speaker the night before the Colorado game. Bloomfield Hills attorney Lou Kasischke had been part of the Everest expedition of 1996, the ill-fated climb documented by Jon Krakauer in his best-seller *Into Thin Air*.

Kasischke had narrowly escaped death in the blizzard that had overtaken the climbers near the summit. Five others in his group had died in the storm. He spoke about determination, reliance on the people who were part of your team, interdependence. He showed them a rope and said that everyone had to grip the same strand and pull each other up for the entire group to reach the top.

The players were spellbound, fascinated by this vigorous, middle-aged man who had dared to climb higher than human beings are supposed to go. Kasischke did not emphasize that three hours from the summit he had been forced to turn back. His group would not have been able to make it to the top and then descend to their camp again within a safe period of time.

Krakauer noted how difficult that decision was. They had spent all that money, time, and energy and then fell short when they were so close to the goal. "And yet faced with a tough decision they were among the few who made the right choice that day," wrote Krakauer. If they had continued to climb, in all likelihood they would have died.

Michigan teams had plenty of experience getting close to the summit. No fewer than seven times under Schembechler, Michigan had started a season 8-0. Each time the top of Everest had been in sight. Yet on every occasion they had been turned away, short of the peak. Once more they could spot it, emerging from the clouds, calling them upward again.

CHAPTER 15

October 18. Michigan 28, Iowa 24

There comes a time in which every good team must fight its way out of a dark place. How well it manages that determines whether it is a great team.

This was Michigan's darkest place of 1997.

It figured to be. Iowa was one of the preseason favorites, ranked no worse than third in the conference. When coach Hayden Fry had the material, he always played Michigan tough. He handed the Wolverines the worst beating of the Schembechler era, a 26-0 pounding at Iowa City in 1984. Over the last fifteen years, Iowa had made the trip to Pasadena more frequently than any Big 10 team besides Michigan: three times. It seemed hard to believe the Hawkeyes had won only eight times in the entire Michigan series, going back to 1900.

They had run up boxcar figures on a weak preseason schedule. Ohio State had defanged them somewhat, beating them soundly.

Still, this figured to be the most formidable offense Michigan had faced.

By half time, Michigan's worst fears had been realized. Going into this game it had given up just two touchdowns and 26 points. At the half, Iowa already had scored three TDs and led 21-7. While the defense was playing well, every part of the Michigan team had broken down at one critical point.

The Wolverines had not given up the big plays this season. This time they gave up three. Iowa's top runner, Tavian Banks, broke off a 53-yard TD run on the defense. Griese, who called this "my worst half of football since I've been here," then threw a 64-yard interception return which quickly led to Iowa's second touchdown. Most shocking, just before the half ended, Michigan's special team let Tim Dwight, the dangerous receiver and kick-return man, get loose on a 61-yard punt return. That was the third TD.

Iowa had put together just 84 yards of offense from scrimmage, but for the first time all year Michigan was looking up at two touchdowns.

To Jon Jansen, right tackle, co-captain, and pivot of the offensive line, this was the defining moment of the season.

"All during the practices and the early games," he said, "Coach Carr kept telling us that every team leaves a mark on the Michigan tradition. 'What is yours going to be?' he asked. This is where we had to find the answer."

For Jansen, the tradition and his place in it was everything.

"There really wasn't a close second choice where I would go to school," he says. "If I'd gone anywhere else my dad would have had to buy a whole new wardrobe. Everything in his closet is maize and blue."

He had grown up in Clawson, a Detroit suburb, where his father was the band director at the middle school.

"The one thing I miss about being on the football team is that I'm not out there when the public address announcer says: 'Band, take the field.' I really like to see them perform. My dad was always talking about how great the Michigan band is. I think it's the biggest reason he became a Michigan football fan.

"But I don't really mean the part about missing the band. The first time I ran out of that tunnel onto the field...that's indescribable. That really is something you can't put into words. That was the most wonderful sensation I'd ever experienced. You hear the cleats on the cement like it was a stampede. Then the light at the end grows bigger and bigger and suddenly you're out on the grass with the noise booming down around you, looking up at these thousands and thousands of faces.

"You know, there's just a certain smell on a football Saturday. I don't know what it is. Leaves and fresh air and the way the locker room smells on game day. There isn't any other smell like it. It's the same wherever you are."

Offensive linemen seem to pick up that scent better than anyone else. Those close to the game insist they are the key to any team. It was the first element Schembechler recruited. "Because if you can't move the ball, you can't do anything," he says. Veteran sportswriters know offensive linemen are generally the most perceptive and articulate members of any team. Most of all, they like to hit people.

"Oh, yes," says Jansen. "That is definitely the appeal. You know that on every play you are going to get to hit somebody. That's what I think of as fun.

"But Zach [Adami] and myself were the only two veterans coming back to our line. We were the only ones who knew what was ahead. It was up to us to use our experience to get the other guys ready. So we talked about it all the time during the summer practices. The necessity of taking your game to another level when the time came. We made those practices as game-like as possible and I still think that was one of the big reasons we were ready.

"And we did have some incentives. We kept hearing talk about how this was going to be a mediocre Michigan team. We really hadn't given them any reason to think any different. We talked about that. Part of the reason everyone on that line came to Michigan was to be part of the winning tradition. It was up to us to get that back.

"I remember coming back out of the tunnel in that Iowa game to start the second half and the fans were just roaring. That was a tremendous boost for us. They didn't think we were out of it. Brian got us out on the field, and he was so calm in the huddle. Just a tower of calm. 'All right,' he said, 'let's get ourselves back in this thing.'"

Carr later called it one of the great comebacks he had seen in college football. Michigan's defense, said Iowa's Banks, "was flying. Ohio State has Andy Katzenmoyer who is flying around on every play. But everyone on the Michigan defense plays like that."

Fry had joked before the game that he'd heard Woodson was going to be covering Dwight. "I'm kind of hopeful they will sic Woodson on Tim because then we'll always know where he is," said Fry. "I may want Dwight to come over and sit on the bench with me and it would be kind of nice to have Charles over there with us."

But in the game, Woodson shut down Iowa's top receiver. He caught one pass for 7 yards. Aside from his one long touchdown run, Banks only gained 46 yards on the ground in 18 carries. Quarterback Matt Sherman completed just 8 of 21 passes.

Meanwhile, Griese finally was getting it cranked up. He hit Russell Shaw for a touchdown pass and then sneaked into the end zone to cap another long march and tie the game. But Iowa had one grenade left to lob. Dwight gathered in the next kickoff and brought it back 72 yards to the Michigan 26. The Wolverines stiffened and Iowa could only get a field goal. But as the fourth quarter began to tick down, Michigan trailed 24-21.

"The ball bounced our way a lot of times during the season," says Jansen. "That's part of it. You've got to have the breaks. But we always seemed to take advantage of ours."

Now came one of the biggest. With Michigan mired at its own 17 yard line, it faced a third and 16. Griese threw to Streets and the ball fell incomplete after a hit by the Iowa defense. As the crowd looked uneasily at the clock to see how much time would be left for the next and final drive, the penalty flag came out. Pass interference. First down Michigan on the 30.

Carr later called this the biggest play of the season. Even if Streets had caught the ball, it appeared as if he would have been tackled immediately—three yards short of a first down. Instead, Griese had all the room he needed. He ran off nine more plays and finally hit Tuman in the end zone from the 9. For the first time all day, Michigan was ahead. Less than three minutes were left on the clock.

But the Hawkeyes suddenly figured out how to move. They needed a touchdown and Sherman found his runner, Banks, on a short pass pattern that gained 30 yards. Suddenly, Iowa was sitting on the Michigan 26.

Sherman was still determined to get the ball to Dwight and called a crossing pattern over the middle, hoping to shake him free of Woodson. Glen Steele came raging in from his end position and Sherman had to throw too soon. The ball landed in the arms of linebacker Sam Sword and he fell to the ground, cradling it.

"Our kids really grew up in that game," said defensive coordinator Herrmann. "Both offense and defense. They never lost their composure. It was something special, the pivotal point in terms of the growth of the team."

For Carr, it simply added to his growing confidence in Griese as a field leader and as a quarterback who was able to execute under pressure. The winning fourth-quarter drive was handled masterfully "because he is a real student of the game," said Carr. "That is an intangible that cannot be measured on a chart. He knows how to react to the situation."

Michigan had come out of its dark place, its scariest challenge. But three hundred miles to the west, something even more stunning had occurred. Unbeaten Michigan State, the team the Wolverines would meet the following week in what they called the toughest stadium in the Big 10 in which to win, had been upended by Northwestern. The battle of two unbeaten powers was not going to happen. Instead, State would take the field at East Lansing in a green and white rage.

CHAPTER 16

Backyard Brawl

If there is one constant element in a Michigan-Michigan State game, it is rage. Over the years, the Ohio State game may have meant more on the Michigan schedule. It comes at the end when the title is on the line. But in terms of incivility and simple dislike, nothing tops State. Even players recruited from other states, and both schools spread a wide net, quickly get into it. More than once, the two teams have engaged in pregame shoving matches in the tunnels. Taunts after a win are common. Fan abuse descends to vicious levels for this one. School officials have expressed concern about the level of hostility over the years and have tried to dampen it when they could. Still, it is part of the landscape in the state of Michigan.

Those who attend the University of Michigan are convinced they won admission to the superior school. They lose no opportunity to remind East Lansing of that, too. "I'm so sick of losing to State," wrote one columnist in the *Michigan Daily* back in the '60s, "that I can't look a cow in the face anymore."

For their part, State supporters would agree fervently with former coach Darryl Rogers' assessment of Michigan as a group of "arrogant asses." Michigan State long ago moved into the ranks of America's great research universities and many of its programs offer undergraduates more direct contact with prestigious faculty than anything at Michigan. Still, State finds it hard to get out from under the label of being second-best. Many of its graduates act as if Michigan were a permanent ingrown toenail on their path of life.

John Hannah, the president of MSU during the late 1940s, was as responsible as anyone for elevating the rivalry. The series began in 1898, and for the next fifty years was as one-sided as it gets. Michigan led 33-6-3. Four of those losses had come during a span in the late '30s when Michigan football was at its lowest ebb. When Hannah came to East Lansing, it was still Michigan State College and played an independent football schedule. Michigan was adamantly opposed to its entering the Big 10. The possibility had been discussed ever since Chicago dropped football in 1939 and reduced the conference to nine teams. But State was kept out.

Hannah felt MSU was poised to go big time in many respects. He was one of the first college presidents to grasp the significance of the GI Bill of Rights, which would pay tuition for World War II veterans. Hannah began building new dormitories without legislative appropriations, figuring correctly that the flood of new students would pay for them. He also decided that it was important to build up the school's athletic reputation, and to accomplish that, he brought in Biggie Munn as football coach.

This occurred at the peak of Michigan dominance. They had beaten the Spartans ten times in a row and rolled to undefeated seasons in 1947 and 1948. But Munn's team played Michigan surprisingly tough during the national championship year of '48, losing only 13-7. The following year it was just 7-3. And in 1950, State finally broke through with a 14-7 victory.

That changed everything. Through the next twenty years, Michigan was 4-14-2 against the Spartans. It was the worst showing, by far, over an extended period against any traditional opponent. The Spartans were national champions in 1952 and finally put together enough votes to crash the Big 10 the following year. Munn, and later Duffy Daugherty, delighted in putting it to Michigan, going to the Rose Bowl three times to Michigan's one between 1954 and 1966. State also was one of the first teams to take advantage of the hard realities of racial segregation. It began recruiting hard in Texas and other southern states for talented black athletes who could not play for major schools at home. They formed the core of State's 1965-66 teams, which won the UPI national championship one year and finished second after playing a legendary tie with undefeated Notre Dame the next.

With the arrival of Schembechler in Ann Arbor, however, the pendulum swung back. After losing his first game to State, he went 17-3. But his rage knew no bounds when State cast one of the votes that kept Michigan out of the 1974 Rose Bowl. Michigan and Ohio State finished that season tied for the conference lead after playing to a 10-10 draw. Since Ohio State had gone to Pasadena the previous year, normal Big 10 policy called for Michigan to be the choice. But the Pac 10 had dominated the series in recent years and Michigan quarterback Dennis Franklin had been injured in the OSU game. There was heavy politicking behind the scenes, hints from the commissioner's office that the conference really had to send its "best" team west to save prestige. In a vote that was supposed to be a formality for Michigan, OSU won. After that, the State game became a vendetta for Bo. Twenty-five years later he is still bitter about what he regards as the worst injustice ever done to one of his teams.

Since 1984, the series also had tightened up. Michigan's advantage had only been 8-5, and in games played at East Lansing it was 3-3. Still State wallowed in frustration. NCAA sanctions after recruiting violations were turned up had kept it out of the Rose Bowl one year. George Perles finally got them to Pasadena in 1988, but then his program quickly came undone. An ugly power struggle resulted in the resignation of the school's highly respected president, John DiBiaggio, and in Perles' dismissal. The damage to the school's academic reputation was severe. Worst of all were the sneers from Ann Arbor.

With the arrival of Nick Saban as head coach, the momentum seemed to be changing. A sense of purpose, of foundation had returned. Saban had trimmed away many hangers-on who had clustered to the football program under Perles. He started bringing in top recruits from Florida and the other new football hotbeds. With a 5-0 start this season it seemed State was at last ready to challenge a Michigan program that appeared to be in decline.

The hype had started building after just a couple of weeks. Northwestern coach Gary Barnett thought that on State's side it might have grown out of control.

"They sure weren't thinking about us," he said after his upset of the Spartans. "I know our kids realized that. I think it helped us." Network TV analysts surmised that Saban had spent a few days of practice working on Michigan rather than on Northwestern.

Saban tried to put a bright face on it. "This game will test this team's character," he said. "How we react after our first loss is a critical test."

Carr professed to be hugely disappointed and said he would have preferred to play an unbeaten Spartan team. But his tears seemed crocodilian. Against a weaker opponent, State had shown surprising vulnerability on defense and inconsistencies in its run-oriented offense. The teams, in fact, almost were mirror images. Powerful runners. Reliance on a short-passing game. Offense designed to minimize mistakes and turn the game over to an overpowering defense.

As media fever raged across the state, it would soon be determined which face of the mirror would crack.

CHAPTER 17

October 25. Michigan 23, Michigan State 7

The game was still rated just about even at kickoff, with no shortage of money on the MSU side. But no one had consulted Charles Woodson about this.

This was the game the cornerback had been pointing for. This was the one he had circled on the calendar.

Two years before, he had played here as a freshman and felt that he, personally, let it get away. As Tony Banks drove the Spartans down the field in the last minutes for the winning touchdown, Woodson had an interception in his hands...and dropped it. It was the edge Banks needed to complete the drive. While Banks completed plenty of other passes over many other defenders, Woodson blamed himself. Now he wanted some payback.

"The feeling after that game, that loss, you can't describe it," he said. "I didn't make the play. I had the game in my hands and I didn't do it. I was not going to let that happen again."

Woodson, instead, made the play that became the best-remembered of Michigan's year. It was so spectacular that for the first time it vaulted him into serious contention for the Heisman Trophy. It didn't decide the game, not as the scoreboard measured things. It simply cut the heart right out of the Spartans at a time when one play could have brought them back into it.

Before it happened, it was clear the commentators had been right. Saban obviously had been working on plays that were installed in the hope of turning Michigan's aggressiveness against them. With Michigan holding an early 3-0 lead, and a State drive bogged down, the Spartans lined up for a field goal. Instead, holder Bill Burke picked up the ball and floated a pass to Sedrick Irvin, State's top running back. There was no one within 15 yards of him. Irvin trotted into the end zone and State had a 7-3 lead.

Woodson characteristically blamed himself for the breakdown in coverage. But there would be no more breakdowns this day. Instead, Michigan slowly, inexorably began to squeeze the life out of the State offense.

"Nobody has been able to run on these guys," said Saban during practice that week. "If you can't do that, you'd better be able to pass. But no one has been able to do that, either."

Saban thought he could. His quarterback, Todd Schultz, was ready to come out firing. Each team would get off 67 plays. Michigan ran 50 times and passed just 17. State had Schultz throwing 38 times and called 29 runs. That ratio was way out of proportion for Michigan State's offense, especially when it was well publicized that the team leading this game in rushing had won twenty-seven of the last twenty-eight times. (The only exception was Banks' passing show in 1995.)

Saban felt that only if Schultz succeeded in driving off the Michigan linebackers could the State runners find enough room to operate. Instead, Woodson seemed to take this game plan as a personal affront.

He was still seething about the '95 game. Then someone told him that in a radio interview during the week one of the Spartans had said Michigan was dead. Oops. Then his mother had called from Ohio to say she heard someone else had remarked that they intended to bottle Charles up on punt returns. So Woodson was in a tizzy, and it grew wilder as the game progressed.

Griese brought Michigan into the lead with a second-quarter drive. State was still within a touchdown, probing for openings, in the third quarter. Schultz went back to pass on third down from his own 20. But with no one open, the quarterback tossed the ball out of bounds to avoid a sack and set up the punt.

Just as the ball reached the sidelines, Woodson came racing into the play. Treating gravity as a mild nuisance, he launched his body in an incredible vertical leap. At its apogee, he managed to get the fingers of his right hand on the ball. Cradling it to his chest as he fell, he kept one foot inside the sideline stripe before returning to earth. As the numbed Spartan Stadium crowd looked on, the Michigan offense came onto the field to put the game away.

As it happened, Carr went conservative and called three running plays. ("Even my wife questioned those calls," he said later, "but I wouldn't change a thing.") They went nowhere and State was still in the game. But Woodson's play seemed to take the pizzazz out of Schultz. State never seriously mounted an offense in the second half. Irvin was shut down. Schultz threw six interceptions. The Spartans never crossed the 50 again until the final minute.

"They did some talking to us in the first quarter and a little bit in the second," said Woodson's backfield companion, Marcus

Ray. "But in the second half, what was there to talk about? They had to use a trick play to score on us."

Ray made it clear real men don't resort to trick plays.

Woodson's second interception of the day led to a clinching fourth-quarter touchdown and Michigan tucked another one away. Afterward, the State players blamed a succession of penalties and mistakes for the loss. They would not concede they had been dominated by a better team. It was essentially the same thing Hayden Fry had said after the Iowa game and Gary Barnett after the Northwestern game: real good defense, sure, but no one had really been stomped. This was not the same faces-ground-in-the-mud feeling opponents were left with in the Schembechler era. Instead, teams lost to Michigan and they weren't sure why. It was annoying.

Woodson conceded the one-handed grab was "probably the best interception I've ever made." Other observers could not recall having seen anything like it. It was replayed constantly on ESPN and the other sports channels.

His two-way talents had won Woodson some attention in 1996, but then it was almost like a novelty act. It resembled the media coverage given to Kordell Stewart when he played both receiver and quarterback for the Pittsburgh Steelers. It was as the British wit Samuel Johnson once observed upon seeing a dancing bear: "The marvel isn't that the thing is done well. The marvel is that it is done at all."

But Woodson also did it well. He was dangerous whenever he came on the field. In the thirty-two-year history of the Heisman Trophy, no primarily defensive player had ever won. (For its first decade everyone played both offense and defense. But the winners were chosen essentially for their offensive skills.) Only two previous winners had not played in the backfield—ends Larry

Kelley of Yale in 1936 and Leon Hart of Notre Dame in 1949. Defensive players usually didn't even finish in the top four of the balloting. Although in many years the best overall college player was undoubtedly a lineman, there didn't seem any way to convince the voters of that. Other trophies had to be established for players at these positions, because they had no realistic shot at the Heisman.

Woodson had caught just five passes, so far, although Carr promised to work him into the offense more often as the weather grew cooler. But he had made a statement in the Michigan State game. In another week he would pronounce himself "the best player in the country standing before you."

There were other statements to be made. Michigan was now 7-0 and ranked number four. Only Nebraska, Penn State, and Florida State were ahead of them, and Penn State was coming up in two weeks.

First there was the matter of Minnesota, another team with which Michigan had something of a history.

CHAPTER 18

November 1. Michigan 24, Minnesota 3

It is a rivalry that has a whiff of mold about it, the kind of scent you come upon in the cellars of damp, old houses.

Once there was nothing like a Michigan-Minnesota game. The Little Brown Jug is the most storied of college football trophies. These were the two most feared teams in the Big 10.

Minnesota once beat Michigan nine times in a row. No one else has even come close to doing that. There are Big 10 schools that haven't beaten Michigan nine times in their entire existence. But that all happened between 1934 and 1942. Minnesota won three national championships in that period. Tom Harmon, for all his glory, never beat the Gophers. If there had been such a thing as television back then that game would have been shown nationally every year.

Since 1967, although the teams meet annually, Minnesota has won just twice. They were 2-27 going into this game. But the two were stingers.

And besides, this was November. Bad things happened to Michigan in November.

In 1977, Schembechler had taken a number-one-ranked team into Minneapolis behind Rick Leach and was beaten, 16-0. It was the only time Leach was shut out in his four years at Michigan.

Nine years later, Michigan was 9-0 going into the Minnesota game. They were ranked second, the game was at Ann Arbor, and Jim Harbaugh was putting up big numbers week after week. Minnesota stopped him, 20-17, and won with a field goal as time expired.

Those were the only two times Minnesota ever beat Bo. Both times it was an arrow through the heart.

Now it was November again. Under Lloyd Carr, the Wolverines' record in August, September, and October was 20-2. In November and beyond it was 4-6.

So far this was a familiar road. But bad things happen in November. Before Carr could truly claim legitimacy as Michigan's coach he had to win in November, too. Minnesota had come within a whisper of upsetting Penn State just two weeks before. Now Carr had to get by this deceptive barrier to begin the final push.

"Tell me what kind of a guy Al Kaline is," he asks a visitor to his office in Schlembecher Hall. "What did he take away from that championship in 1968 that was important in his life? That's what I want to know. I remember the day the Tigers won it. I had my first teaching job, phys ed at a little school on the east side of Detroit. I had to drive through downtown on the way home to Riverview and we got caught up in the celebration. Everyone was so happy, because what the Tigers accomplished that year was such a satisfying story.

"I think that's why so many people found satisfaction in what we did in 1997. Don't forget these are just kids out there. I know I'm criticized sometimes for being overly protective of my players. But, what the hell, they're just young guys. Any decision I make is based on what's best for them. When it comes right down to it there are more important things than winning a championship. I know expectations are high. But this place, this university is 180 years old and a football championship has to be measured against what that means."

Carr comes out from behind his desk to sit in a chair beside his questioner. His office is sparely furnished. A poster of the championship team hangs behind the desk. He is now in constant demand. He had to cancel a previous appointment when he was asked to stay a few hours longer than he had intended at a charity golf outing in Grand Rapids—to shake hands, press the flesh, let the glow settle in. The previous night he had been handing out awards at a banquet in Petoskey. Everyone wants Lloyd Carr in this post-championship spring. A warm, crinkly-eyed individual who has kept an athlete's bearing, he looks like the role he fills.

"I let the captains run the last meeting before the season begins," says Carr. "I knew they were sick of hearing it. They were sick of talking about the four-loss seasons and sick of being told the program was in a downturn. It motivated them. It bonded them in a way that's hard to measure. That's what pulled us through the Notre Dame game. Three times we got ourselves into positions where we could have lost that game. But the tenacity of these guys wouldn't allow that.

"To me Brian Griese is the symbol of that team. Does anyone really know what he went through? He comes here without a scholarship. He wins the job and then he loses it. He constantly hears that the team will never win if he is the quarterback because he doesn't have the physical tools.

"But he never loses sight of his goals. He follows his dream. If people keep hearing about what they can't do, sometimes they start to believe it. He never did. He was relentless and when he came through the tough times there wasn't too much that was going to shake him. After what I saw Brian Griese accomplish last year, if I ran a pro team I would have drafted him in a heartbeat."

You wonder how much of himself Carr saw in Griese. Carr was an all-state quarterback in Riverview and was heavily recruited. He chose Missouri but found himself as a backup on a team strong enough to go to the Sugar Bowl. With little chance to become a starter, he transferred to Northern Michigan. He began all over again and took the team to an undefeated season. There was no promise of a Sugar Bowl at the end of a season at Northern Michigan. But even then Carr felt there were more important things.

"The game has changed," he says. "People keep asking why Michigan finally switched to an attacking defense. The philosophy here had always been that you didn't give up the big play. But you have to understand that the rules changed. They now favor the offense. They give smaller, faster guys the advantage. We had to change, too, and we got faster. The attacking defense was a result of that.

"There is also less emphasis on the option. Except for a handful of programs, running the option is almost a mark of weakness. Most Big 10 schools are recruiting the big, tough quarterback who can throw from the pocket. So in that situation a pro-type defense, where you sell out on the possibility of an option, can work. That was our model. We weren't afraid to take chances or make mistakes. For this defense to work the kids have to play hard all the time. No peaks and valleys. We knew we had a group of kids we could count on to do that."

The Minnesota game was surprisingly unsurprising. Minnesota took the opening kickoff, marched 71 yards, kicked a field goal, and was never heard from again.

The Gophers finished with 102 yards in offense and six first downs. They didn't complete a pass in the second half. "That is the best college defense I have ever seen," said Minnesota coach Glen Mason afterward.

Woodson scored on a 33-yard reverse, his first rushing touchdown of the year, to give Michigan the lead. After that, the gap steadily widened.

A few days later Woodson stated he was the best player in all the land.

"If I was Charles," said Sam Sword, "I would have said the same thing."

CHAPTER 19

Facing Joe Pa

Many years ago, one of Bear Bryant's Alabama teams was getting ready to make its first trip into State College and play Penn State. Bryant had heard about tough traffic conditions leading in and out of the place on two-lane roads winding through the mountains. So he called Joe Paterno.

"Joe," he said, "we're gonna have some problems getting back to Harrisburg to catch our jet after the game. Could you call the governor and ask him to have the state police clear a lane for our buses?"

Paterno listened and replied: "Paul, we just don't do things like that here."

That's the way it is in Happy Valley. They keep it as simple and unchanging as the basic white uniforms worn by the Nittany Lions. They have won two national championships under Paterno. The stadium is the third largest on a college campus.

Paterno, or Joe Pa as he is known across the length and breadth of Pennsylvania, is such a popular figure that he seriously contemplated a political career back in the '80s.

In the larger scheme of things, it was only football. Paterno seriously says that his goal at Penn State was to turn its program into "the Michigan of the East, because we are an eastern school built along the lines of the great state universities of the Midwest. That's why the Big 10 was a great fit for us. We also felt that by joining we would elevate football in the East."

Instead, almost the opposite occurred. The addition of Penn State seemed to raise the national status of the conference. All at once, there was a third dominant team in the Big 10, a conference perceived to be sliding in terms of comparative national strength. Ironically, joining the conference even may have cost Paterno a third national title. His undefeated 1994 team led the Big 10 in its second year of play there and was obligated to go to the Rose Bowl. It was matched against a lackluster Oregon team, which it defeated easily. But it had lost the chance to challenge unbeaten Nebraska for the national title in the Orange Bowl. Nebraska finished at number one; Penn State number two—even though there was a large body of opinion that Paterno's team may have had the most versatile college offense in years.

On three earlier occasions, however, Penn State also had gone through the year undefeated and didn't win the national title. The knock on them then was that they played a soft eastern schedule. Go figure.

In fact, Paterno probably lost the 1994 national title in the Indiana game. Having run up a big lead, he rested his starters in the fourth quarter and Indiana scored two late, meaningless touchdowns. But the masterminds who vote in the polls saw that Indiana had beaten the spot and moved Nebraska into the lead.

As far as Paterno was concerned, it wasn't an issue. "There are more important things than winning championships," he says, an almost verbatim expression of Carr's guiding philosophy. Coaches are supposed to say things like that. But Paterno and Carr seem to mean it.

Joe Pa was now seventy years old. He had been at Penn State since 1966, prowling the sidelines with his scowl, his dark glasses, his suit, and white socks. His team had been the preseason number-one pick and had beaten Ohio State in a strong, come-from-behind win against a top defense. The Lions had struggled against Minnesota and Northwestern, however, and were currently ranked number two. Moreover, for the first time in three years Paterno would not have a week off to get ready for the Michigan game. That had been a sore point in Ann Arbor, and there was much grumbling over how a supposedly neutral computer could always spit out a schedule giving Paterno that extra week. But not this time.

"We don't have to prepare for them; they have to prepare for us," shrugged Penn State fullback Anthony Cleary. It was not meant to sound arrogant. It was a simple statement of fact. In its fifth year in the conference, the Penn State game had become a biggie for every school.

"We have to respect them," admitted Griese. "We've given them no reason to respect us."

Penn State had knocked off Michigan three straight times, and in the last two years it had been in convincing fashion. They were undebatable whippings, 27-17 and 29-17.

For his part, Joe Pa seemed to have turned into Juan Ponce de León. He had found the fountain of youth.

"The Big 10 has been a tremendous stimulant for me," he said. "It's what gets me up in the morning. I'm a competitor and I enjoy a challenge. That doesn't mean I can handle it, but I look forward to it."

He had started off as an undersized quarterback at Brown and led a school that, even by Ivy League standards, was not noted for its strong athletic tradition to two championships. In the words of the great New York sportswriter Stanley Woodward: "He can't run and he can't throw. All he can do is think and win." Paterno had considered a career in law. But the opportunity to assist Rip Engle took him to Penn State and he never left.

Over the years, many had tried to puncture the legend. A few former players described him as arbitrary, brusque, and dictatorial. Others claimed that his real genius lay in selecting brilliant assistants who stuck with him through the years.

Nonetheless, Paterno was the most respected coaching mind in the country, and he almost never lost at Happy Valley.

The networks had a field day building it up, in the manner of a bad heavyweight fight. They called it Judgment Day. This Saturday was not only Michigan and Penn State playing for the Rose Bowl and a possible national title. It was also third-ranked Florida State playing similarly unbeaten North Carolina for the ACC title and national ranking.

The Nebraska-Missouri game was not deemed worthy of inclusion in Judgment Day. The top-ranked Cornhuskers were not expected to break a sweat against a program that had been somnolent for years. As it turned out, however, the events in Columbia, Missouri, would be among the most significant of the afternoon.

In the Michigan-Penn State game, the experts liked Penn State. Home field. Proven coach. Confident team.

Quarterback Mike McQueary said that Penn State had played tougher games in the fourth quarter and that could mean the difference. As for the self-acknowledged best player in the country, McQueary had no problem with Charles Woodson.

"We're Penn State and we're not the kind of team that shies away from a particular player," said McQueary. "We'll go right at him. You can't go around him or hope to avoid him and cut off half the field on yourself. We'll be careful with the ball and know what he can do. He's a great athlete and a great corner, but certainly we're going to challenge him."

As it turned out, McQueary was not going to be in the position to challenge anybody. Not on this Judgment Day.

CHAPTER 20

November 8. Michigan 34, Penn State 8

By the end of the first quarter you could walk down Church Street in Ann Arbor and hear the screaming coming from every house. Any student who couldn't make the trip to State College was in front of a television set. And they couldn't believe what they were seeing.

Everybody knew the Michigan defense was good. But no one could have dreamed it was this good. It took an offense averaging 465 yards a game and blew it to smithereens. Aside from an occasional burst by its great running back, Curtis Enis, the Lions were helpless. Everything they tried was demolished.

Michigan had taken the kickoff and moved close enough for a field goal. Penn State then got the ball on its own 25. Offensive coordinator Fran Gantner tried to do what seemed logical: make Michigan's defensive aggressiveness work against itself.

His first scripted play was a pass off a fake reverse. Michigan, meanwhile, had shifted just before the snap into a five-man rush, a defensive alignment used with devastating success by the Chicago Bears during their Super Bowl season of 1985. The offensive line, believing it had all rushers accounted for, found itself overwhelmed. Before quarterback McQueary could turn from the fake reverse, Glen Steele was on top of him. He yanked the quarterback to the ground for a 10-yard loss.

All at once, it was very quiet at Happy Valley. And on Church Street, the noise rolled in waves from every open window.

After a running play, McQueary tried again. This was a simple dropback pass, but this time Juaquin Feazell was on top of him at once. Seven-yard loss.

Right there, it was finished. McQueary never seemed able to recover psychologically from this initial onslaught. He would pass for just 68 yards, convert no third downs. He played tentatively, as if he fully expected to have Michigan players dropping on him from the sky every time he moved.

The Michigan offense seemed to feed off what it saw happening on the field. Using the ball-control game plan to perfection, Griese took them down the field one time after another. First it was Anthony Thomas racing in from the 12. Then it was Woodson coming in to grab a 33-yard scoring pass. Then it was Griese finding his favorite target, Tuman, from the 8.

By half time it was 24-0, the biggest lead ever run up against a Paterno team at home.

But it didn't stop there. Chris Howard burst open on a 29-yard dash. Then a field goal. Now it was 34-0. The Michigan offensive line was ripping huge holes in the Lions' defense. Howard finished with 120 yards and even Griese, not the nimblest runner around, got 46. When he passed, Griese was 14 of 22, picking the secondary apart with his quick, surgical strikes.

Finally, with nothing left to dispute, Penn State scored. It was the first touchdown Michigan had allowed all year in the second half.

"We didn't like that," said Marcus Ray. "We really, really didn't like that. But honestly, this wasn't easy. It was a matter of preparation. We came in here prepared to dominate."

"It didn't get any better than the Penn State game," says Sword. "We gave them absolutely nothing to cheer about. That was the culmination. All year long the coaches had been challenging us. They kept talking about the fifty-year reunion of the 1948 Rose Bowl team. 'They're going to be there,' Coach Carr kept saying. 'The question is are you going to be there?' At Penn State, it all came together, everything we'd been working for all our careers."

Sword was another Michigan player who had overcome an early mistake. As a freshman he was involved in the unauthorized use of a credit card. He was suspended from the team and barred from spring practice.

"That was a silly thing," he says now. "But it opened a door. It let me know that I wasn't this big, bad person who could get away with whatever [I] wanted. Football was almost taken away from me and next to my daughter and my family that is the thing I love most.

"When I'm on the football field, it's like my quiet zone. I love the smash-mouth, the physical game, being out there and knowing they're coming after you."

As the shocked Penn State crowd filed out, Dhani Jones found his parents in the middle of a few thousand Michigan fans who had made the trip. To acknowledge their support, they were standing along the front row of the stadium, cheering and high-fiving the players who passed in front of them.

"Emotionally, that was the peak for me," Jones says. "Where I grew up, not far from the Maryland campus, Penn State was always the natural rivalry. We had a fury to win that day. The personal motivation was higher than it's ever been.

"It was my dad's fiftieth birthday and my parents came up with a busload of thirty-five people. They were all chanting 'Dee-fense, D-Jones.' Unreal."

Even before the final gun, supposedly blasé Ann Arbor had gone crazy. The crowds were forming on South University Street, the commercial strip closest to most residential areas and a traditional gathering place for celebration. Soon the students had blocked traffic and were on the move to the west. A few blocks away, directly in their path, Lee Bollinger and his wife were watching the final minutes of the game on TV in the president's house.

"I remember thinking to myself what an exciting moment this was," Bollinger says. "The team played so much better than anyone had expected. The struggle had proven their fortitude and there was a sense of elation.

"Then the doorbell rang and my wife told me I had better come out and take a look. There was a throng of a few thousand students out there, asking for me to come out and say a few words. I had never anticipated anything like this. It was clear to me that this was a very special moment.

"There had been a physics symposium on campus earlier in the day and from an academic standpoint that was certainly the more significant event. And yet you have to realize that there are moments worthy of respect that really have nothing to do with the scholastic life on campus. These students wanted to share one of those moments with me and I was deeply touched. We had just redecorated the house upon moving in, but there was such happiness in that group that I impulsively invited all of them to come in.

"I don't think I'd do that again. But at that time it was unquestionably the right thing to do."

Those who remained in front of their TVs saw an equally compelling drama taking place in Missouri. Nebraska had been played off its feet by this deep underdog for most of the game and was desperately trying to rally. With time running out, quarterback Scott Frost threw into the end zone, a pass that appeared to be falling incomplete. But a Nebraska receiver kicked the ball just before it hit the ground and on the rebound a teammate made the catch. Nebraska had tied the score. The kick seemed to have been deliberate and the Nebraska player admitted as much afterward. The proper call was a penalty. But the officials never made it and Nebraska won the game in overtime.

The voters in the AP poll were convinced. Michigan jumped three places and was now number one, although Florida State took over that position in the USA Today/CNN tally. It was the first time they had topped the rankings since October 1990. Not since 1976 had they been ranked first in November. And the time before that was in the championship season of 1948.

Only one thing had marred the perfection of the day. Early in the first quarter, junior defensive back Daydrion Taylor had come racing upfield to stop a Penn State screen pass. The hitting had been fierce up to that point. But this collision was frightening. Ball carrier and tackler met helmet-to-helmet and both players staggered back. Then they fell to the ground, both of them knocked unconscious.

"I have never seen anything close to that kind of hit," says Sword. "I thought I'd been in some tough football games, but that was unbelievable. It sounded like a cannon shot to me. I had this wild kind of feeling when I saw it, like I wanted to hit somebody myself.

"But then I looked down at Daydrion and my heart just sank."

"I hated seeing that," says Carr. "I had visited Daydrion's family down in Texas when we were recruiting him and I thought about his mother when he was lying there. It was a tremendous sense of relief when we heard that he was OK.

"But he had always played the game totally without fear. When I visited him in the hospital after that game, he was afraid. That was hard to take, one of the scariest things I've seen. Here we were at one of the greatest points of the season and this kid was fighting through the unknown. Thank God, things turned out OK. He won't play football again but he will finish school.

"I try to tell people that there are more important things than football. This was one of them."

Taylor is a coach's assistant with the 1998 Wolverines.

In just a few weeks, football fans in Michigan would see the nightmarish scene repeated: Detroit Lions linebacker Reggie Brown, stretched out on the field with a severe neck injury that also would end his career and nearly his life.

They were chilling reminders what sort of game football has become. The players get bigger and faster every year. Three-hundred pounders run like sprinters. Advances in equipment can't keep pace. Every time a player takes the field he knows, at some level of consciousness, that the game—and much, much more—can end for him on any play. He tries to block it from his mind because he cannot play the game afraid. But sometimes the worst fears come true, even as his team moves to the top of the world.

CHAPTER 21

November 15. Michigan 26, Wisconsin 16

One is a dangerous number. In the forty-nine years since their last championship, Michigan had held that spot in the AP poll for just seventeen weeks. Eight of them came consecutively in 1976, before that 8-0 team was upended by Purdue, 16-14. The Wolverines held on to the slot four more weeks in 1977 and then were beaten by Minnesota, 16-0. Since that time, the stays at the top had been brief and unhappy. Michigan was the number-one pick in the 1981 preseason poll, then lost the opener at Wisconsin. In Moeller's first season, 1990, no sooner did they climb to first than they were knocked off by Michigan State, 28-27. It had been seven years and twenty-six days since they had been this far up the slope of Everest.

Moreover, none of those four losses by a number-one Michigan team had been to a ranked opponent.

"You never say you are the number-one team in the nation

until after the season," advised Schembechler from hard experience. "Don't listen to the polls. Don't watch the polls. Don't care about the polls."

Five consecutive years, from 1970 to 1974, Bo had gone into the last game of the year unbeaten. Three times he lost to Ohio State, once he tied, and, most bitterly, he lost to Stanford in the 1972 Rose Bowl on a field goal with sixteen seconds to go.

"And the funny thing was that not one of those times did we go into that game ranked number one," he says. "We go through all those seasons unbeaten and the best we ever were at the end was third. Everyone on the TV networks was convinced that the power was in the Southeastern Conference and the Big 8 in those years. You can't fight the networks. So when people ask if it bothered me that I never finished number one, I have to say I don't think we ever really had a fair chance to get there.

"In 1970 we go down to Columbus and because of the no-repeat rule for the Rose Bowl we had no chance of going anywhere. And Woody [Hayes] is steamed over us beating him the year before. So what incentive did we have? Then in '73 we tie them when we're ranked fourth and OSU is number one. That's the year we got screwed by the conference vote on the bowl team. Southern California has one of the weakest Rose Bowl teams in their history. We would have killed 'em. But we stay home and we drop two spots in the final ratings. We're 10-0-1 and they rank us sixth.

"Then there was that damn Rose Bowl with Stanford. They beat us on a fake punt that we'd practiced against and yelled from the sidelines that it was coming. But even if we'd won that game, Nebraska wins the title. They beat Oklahoma in that big showdown at the end of the season and they had the title won by acclamation. So we were really never in the position that these guys in '97 were in late in the season."

But if one is a dangerous number, ten is a dangerous week.

Coming off an emotional win at Penn State. Just before the annual frenzy with Ohio State. And going into Madison to play a big, nasty 8-2 Wisconsin team looking for someone to crunch.

Carr had interviewed for the Wisconsin job in 1989. Instead, the Badgers picked Notre Dame assistant Barry Alvarez. The choice had worked out well. One of the toughest Big 10 football programs in the '50s and early '60s had gone slack and soft. Wisconsin had not been back to Pasadena since 1963. But under Alvarez they returned to the basics and were capable of playing smash-mouth with anybody.

Wisconsin won the conference championship in 1993. And when they beat Michigan that year for just the second time in twenty-four games, Camp Randall Stadium went up for grabs. Several students were trampled in the postgame rush onto the field and Madison, always noted for its jubilant mode of celebration, outdid itself that evening. Alvarez then beat Michigan soundly in Ann Arbor the next year. They had not met since then.

Wisconsin was still alive in this Big 10 season. Alvarez had pulled his team back together after a preseason bowl battering by Syracuse. Since then they had lost only to surprising Purdue and were ranked twenty-third. With wins over Michigan and Penn State in the last two games, Wisconsin could be heading back to Pasadena.

There was bound to be one game along the way in which the Michigan defense was going to be rocked. This one was it. After holding every team but Notre Dame to 101 yards or less rushing, Michigan found itself gasping for air in Madison.

"That was the most physical game I ever played in," says Sam Sword. "There was no chance that we were going to let down our focus. We had talked about that all week; getting so close now, we can't overlook this game. We knew it would be a rowdy atmosphere up there and that they would fight us to the end.

"But I'll tell you they brought everything they had. That was the hardest anyone played us all year. I was just happy to get out of there."

Carr agreed that the ten-point margin wasn't the story.

"Our quarterback coach, Stan Parrish, said that might have been the best game he ever was involved in," says Carr. "It was real football weather, cold and blustery. You were fighting the elements along with Wisconsin. You can't know how much fun that is until you're in it."

Schembechler could see that Alvarez had studied the attacking Michigan defense better than any other coach so far and had an idea about how to work against it.

"He started running the option," says Bo, "and I was afraid that would happen somewhere down the line. When you commit your end and outside linebacker to the rush, that leaves only an inside linebacker to cover the quarterback and the trailer on an option with no backup. A good option quarterback can hang that guy out to dry."

Michigan had jumped off fast to a 14-0 lead, on a short TD run by Chris Howard and a 38-yard strike from Griese to Tai Streets. It was his first reception in three games as the receiver had tried to play through injuries.

But Wisconsin started to move, closing the gap to 17-10.

"This time it was our offense's turn to win a game for us," says Carr. "They stood up at a time when we were struggling on defense. Brian had to keep the ball out of their hands because they were moving it on us."

Once again, with the game on the line Griese handled the short-pass, ball-control game perfectly. He finished with 20 out of 27 for 282 yards, just 2 yards short of his high total of the year. He hit Streets five times, Shaw and Howard on four occasions. Woodson came in and caught three passes. He threw to six receivers in all. Griese even caught one himself, as the endlessly versatile Woodson took a lateral from him and then hit his quarterback on a 28-yard completion.

Michigan had clinched a share of the conference championship, but there was still much business to attend to. One team still could spoil the planned reunion with the 1948 Rose Bowl squad in Pasadena. Ohio State week was here, and a stadium full of ghosts would have to be exorcised.

CHAPTER 22

We're From O-HIO

Tad Jones once addressed his Yale team before the year's biggest game. "Gentlemen," he said, "you are about to take the field against Harvard. You will never again in your lives do anything this important."

No coach has ever said that before a Michigan-Ohio State game. No one had to. It was understood. This is why the players who went to those schools made their decision. To play in this game.

"They made such a big thing about beating Michigan in Columbus," said Marcus Ray, who had grown up there. "I figured if it was all that important I should go to Michigan."

Woody Hayes wouldn't even mention its name. To him it was always, "That school up north." One of the best-known tunes in the Buckeye repertoire goes: "We don't give a damn for the whole state of Michigan...We're from O-HIO." Coaches rose and fell at

Columbus over their ability to get the job done against Michigan. It was Hayes' delight to run up the score on the Wolverines whenever he could. There was rioting along High Street in Columbus after one especially satisfying victory in 1955, when it was still a novelty to beat Michigan. Even now, visitors in Columbus from Michigan on game day are advised to park so the license plate doesn't show.

There are no more loyal and enthusiastic fans on the planet than Ohio State's. Columbus is now the biggest city in Ohio, and until the National Hockey League puts an expansion team there in 2000 it remains the largest metropolitan area in the country without big league pro sports. No matter. The Buckeyes are everything here. Lane Street after a game is the biggest open-air party in the Midwest.

Even though Michigan played in the larger stadium, OSU outdrew them consistently throughout the '50s and '60s, selling out weekly and leading the nation in attendance. With the arrival of Canham and his marketing techniques, however, that changed. In 1974, Michigan outdrew OSU for only the third time in twenty-three seasons. It has never trailed them since. That also rankles in Columbus.

Under Hayes, Ohio State dominated the series. It went 15-6-1 against Michigan between 1954 and 1975. For Michigan, however, before the coming of Schembechler it was just one of many big games on the schedule. Michigan State would always outdraw OSU. There was the Little Brown Jug to fight over and Illinois was an important tradition. But for Ohio State, only one game mattered. It wasn't a game. It was a crusade.

Schembechler had studied under Hayes, learned his coaching philosophy, sought to emulate him. The first thing that greets visitors to Bo's office even today, opposite the front door, is a drawing of Schembechler and Hayes. Under Bo, the game was elevated to a level of importance only slightly below what it had always occupied in Columbus.

There was never a time in the ten games the two men coached against each other that one team or the other was not ranked in the Top 10. On seven occasions, they both were. No other team from the Big 10 besides these two went to the Rose Bowl between 1968 and 1981. Michigan-Ohio State was always the championship and the trip to California.

But that also had worked against the reputation of the Big 10. As Schembechler complained, despite five straight years in which he went into the last game of the year unbeaten and untied, not once was he ranked number one. (Ohio State was ranked number one going into this game three times. In 1969, they lost. In 1973, they tied. In 1976, they won and then lost in the Rose Bowl.) To the rest of the country, it was the Big 8 and Little 2. How can you take a conference seriously when there was just one big game on the schedule? Moreover, during this same period of dual dominance, Michigan and OSU were 3-10 in the Rose Bowl. The last Big 10 team to win a national championship had been OSU in 1968.

Earle Bruce, despite taking Ohio State to two Rose Bowls, never felt accepted in Columbus because he was only a .500 coach against Michigan. One of the big reasons John Cooper was hired to replace him was because his Arizona State team had beaten Michigan in the 1987 Rose Bowl. But since Cooper's arrival in 1988 things had not gone well. In the previous nine games between the teams, Michigan was 7-1-1. It was widely rumored that Cooper was out before he managed to tie a favored Michigan team in Columbus in 1992. The noose was so tight, though, that Cooper stalked out of the postgame news conference when someone asked if he thought his job was now safe.

Worst of all, for the last two years, Michigan had spoiled the entire Ohio State season. Both years OSU came into the game ranked second. In 1995, Michigan beat them 31-23 and took them out of the Rose Bowl. In 1996, they beat them 13-9 and denied them a national championship.

Now the roles were reversed. Now, at last, it was Michigan at number one and Ohio State cast as the spoiler. The Buckeyes had lost at Penn State, but since then had squished everything in their path. For the first time since 1986, both teams were in the Top 10. The Buckeyes were ranked fourth and speeding like a torpedo through a scarlet sea of revenge.

"I don't think the players individually hate each other," says Ray. "It's not about that. This is a game. It's not life or death. But I think it's got to be a mental block with them. It's there, although they make excuses and say it's something else. But it will be there until they beat us."

"I'm just going to have fun," said Griese. "I've been through two of these before. No need to be nervous or uptight. I'm going to enjoy myself."

"We don't need to say anything," said Glen Steele. "We don't need to talk. We go out and practice all week long and then go out and play on Saturday."

But Ohio State had not yet learned the virtue of silence. Over the last two years, some OSU players had remarked that the Michigan game was no big deal anymore; that there were now much tougher teams on their schedule. This year Ohio State's top receiver, Glenn Boston, decided to speak up.

During game week, he opined that he already had faced a couple of cornerbacks as good as Charles Woodson. In fact, said Boston, his own teammate, Antonio Wingfield, was a better corner than Woodson.

Earlier in the season, Woodson had suggested that coaches might want to keep a tighter rein on what their players said before a game. Both Michigan State and Penn State had made it clear they did not intend to make special provisions for Woodson. Then they paid for it.

"Everybody sees what Boston said," said Woodson. "Everybody reads it and everybody takes it to heart. That's just to our advantage. He just called us out. Some people are going to have to step up and show him what team is all about."

Woodson's buddy Ray promised him privately that he would settle accounts with Boston. But Woodson said he "was biting my tongue."

Besides, the time for talk was over. It was Michigan-Ohio State with everything on the line; just as it had been before, just as it should be. Across two states, everything came to a stop.

Another timeless football Saturday in Ann Arbor. But not in recent memory had there been one like this. In the chill of a November morning, as the throng made its way through the streets to the big stadium, the last measure of drama and emotion was about to be played out.

CHAPTER 23

November 22. Michigan 20, Ohio State 14

Even those who had not missed a home game in twenty or twenty-five years could not remember an atmosphere like this. It wasn't just the size of the crowd. At 106,982 it was the biggest in stadium history. But truthfully, once you get that many in the place, who can tell the difference?

Size matters, but there was something else, too. This was the sort of sensation that may come once in a lifetime: a mixture of foreboding and anticipation, of dread and elation. Even the most stolid Old Blue in the stands felt his stomach flipping around like a teenager today. Everything was vivid and charged.

"The Victors" was sung with extra verve. The band was cheered with special vigor. Every routine announcement brought nervous laughter. And when the team finally charged out of the tunnel, leaping to touch the banner at the middle of the field, everyone stood up to cheer—to cheer wildly for a moment they thought would never come. It was a moment many of them feared had been consigned to the history books. They were ready to board the roller coaster for the ride of a lifetime.

At the stadium and across the country, wherever Michigan alumni had gathered on this Saturday, they felt their hands grow ice cold. All other images and sounds faded off to form a distant hum.

Ohio State was always dangerous. But now they were playing as well as any team in the country. Their defense was anchored by linebacker Andy Katzenmoyer, acknowledged to be the best in the conference. Boston really had not been bragging too much. Antonio Wingfield was an outstanding cornerback. The Buckeyes could not mount a defensive rush as furious as Michigan's front. But they could stop anybody.

On offense, they had an outstanding runner in Pepe Pearson and a top receiver in Boston. Moreover, Ohio State came at you with two different looks. Their starting quarterback, Stanley Jackson, ran the option; Wisconsin had shown what an option quarterback could do against the Michigan defense. But Joe Germaine was regarded as far more dangerous, with the best long passing touch in the Big 10.

Everyone also knew how badly OSU wanted this game. To break up Michigan's perfect season would be the best payback imaginable. It would wipe away the sting of many defeats. Rugged Wisconsin had been a good lead-in to this game. But this was the real thing.

The teams probed throughout the first quarter. Michigan could not move at all, while OSU managed at least one first down each time they had the ball. Late in the quarter, Jackson started the Buckeyes heading into Michigan territory. But on a first down at the Wolverines 33, the front broke through on him for the first time, rattled him to the ground, and shook the ball loose. With that play something seemed to click.

Griese finally started a drive after the fumble, and although a penalty blunted that one he started moving them again on the first possession of the second quarter. After an exchange of punts, Michigan took over on its 38.

A quick pass to tight end Aaron Shea and a Chris Howard burst got a first down. Then on third and 11, Woodson came into the game. Ohio State sensed what was coming and called for a linebacker blitz. As the rusher broke through, Chris Floyd met him with a block that straightened him up and gave Griese some time. Carr pointed out later that it wasn't even Floyd's blocking assignment on that set. But because of the block, Griese found Woodson, who streaked to the Ohio State 16.

It was the first threat of the day, and Floyd took the hand-off on the next play and bulled up the middle to the 1. One play later, Thomas was in the end zone. 7-0 Michigan. While no one could have guessed it, that was to be the last time the Michigan offense would be a factor in this game.

OSU got the ball back and this time Germaine was harried, unable to set up, dropped for a 10-yard loss. On third and 16, OSU punted from its own 21 yard line. Waiting at his own 22 was Woodson. The return had been called for wall left and a line of blockers was set up for him. He dodged once, eluded another tackler with a stagger step, and then he was behind the wall.

"You could see it happening all the way," said Tom DeLisle, sitting in the same seats he had occupied for fifteen years with his close friend Tom Ryan. The two men had been partners on a morning-drive-time radio show years before in Detroit. While both were graduates of the University of Detroit, like so many others around the state they long ago had adopted Michigan as their team.

"I had never heard a sound like that before at the stadium. It was as if the place had levitated. People were screaming by the time Woodson reached the 50 because we could all see there was nothing in front of him. It was an unbelievable moment. All those years of coming out to Ann Arbor for those games...it had all been for this."

Woodson was mobbed as his jubilant teammates poured into the end zone. All across America you could practically hear the Heisman ballots being switched. But he wasn't through. Not on this day.

Ohio State ran six more plays in the half, got nowhere, and left the field trailing 13-0. But they were hardly beaten. With Jackson running the offense, they took the second-half kickoff and started coming right down the field. A pass to tight end Dee Miller brought it to the 9, and a running play took the ball to the 7. On second down, Jackson dropped back, looking for Miller cutting across the field. Woodson sized up the pattern and dashed in front of the receiver. He landed in the end zone with the ball and the threat was over.

Woodson had done everything a player could do: set up one TD on a pass reception, scored another on a punt return, stopped a third with an interception. He had taken over the game of the year.

Michigan punted after three plays and OSU prepared to move again from its own 45. Jackson dropped back to pass on first down, knowing the only way to beat the Michigan defense was to get yards early in the series of downs. But the rush was right in his face again. Instead of taking the loss, he fluttered the ball to the side. Andre Weathers picked it off in full stride and galloped

43 yards down the sideline to score. Another big play, and it was 20-0.

But the celebration was premature. Ohio State would be conceding nothing. Not in a Michigan game. Not today. That is not how this series is played. Ever.

Another OSU series went nowhere and Germaine came back in the game. A run, a pass to Miller, and then he spotted Boston, racing free behind Woodson. Germaine hit him with a perfect pass and Boston turned to wave the ball in Woodson's face as he crossed the goal line. He had his moment, but it was still a 20-7 game.

Then the machine started to wobble. Thomas ended a drive by fumbling at midfield as the quarter came to a close. OSU had to punt and Griese started the team from their own 9. On third and 3, the unflappable quarterback finally made a mistake. He was blind-sided by an OSU tackler and fumbled. Ohio State had the ball on the Michigan 2.

Pearson took one play to reach the end zone and now it was 20-14 with almost the entire fourth quarter to play. The mood of exultation had swung back. Suddenly it was a game again and Ohio State seemed to be gaining confidence with every minute. Could they be held out again?

The Michigan drive stalled at the 43 and Ohio State started coming again. Pearson battered away for four straight runs, and now it was first down on the Michigan 40. Pearson got it again, but suddenly Josh Williams broke through from his end position and put him down for a 5-yard loss. As the defensive unit leaped on Williams in a frenzy, the noise again rolled through the stadium.

Ohio State didn't know it, but they were done. Williams' play sealed it. They would run eight more plays in this game for a net loss of 7 yards. Forced to pass, Germaine went 1 for 6 and could not get free of the ferocious Michigan rush. At one point, Ray, true to his promise to Woodson, undercut Boston and sent him cartwheeling through the air to land sprawling on the turf. The shot made the cover of *Sports Illustrated* under the headline: "Take That!"

With the seconds ticking off, a final pass fell incomplete at the OSU 17. Michigan took over, ran two plays, and it was done.

Before the players could reach the sidelines, the students had come over the side. The Michigan students, usually way too cool to lose it over something like a football game, came screaming out of their section in the northwestern corner of the stands. A few Ann Arbor cops swung their clubs wildly at the first wave and then were simply overwhelmed.

The players swarmed to the sidelines, gathered in a huddle, and started to sing "The Victors." The students joined in, hugging each other and jumping up and down. There were roses and some players dashed into the crowd holding the flowers in their teeth. Then they rushed back to the sidelines to start the team cheer: "It's great to be a Michigan Wolverine."

Jon Jansen went into the stands to look for his parents. "They were laughing and crying and we all hugged," he says. "It was the most amazing feeling of my life to see my dad, who was such a huge Michigan fan, sharing this moment with me."

And still the big crowd didn't want to go home. It had taken forty-nine years for this; most weren't even that old. They wouldn't leave until they had savored every moment, soaked in this vista of Michigan Stadium so they would remember it for a lifetime.

In a few more hours, it would become even sweeter. Florida

would upset Florida State. Michigan was going to be the undisputed number-one team in America, ranked first in both major polls.

The Wolverines were going to the Rose Bowl to play for the national championship. The tradition had been reborn. It couldn't get any better than this.

CHAPTER 24

Trophy Time

For the first time all year, Charles Woodson didn't know what to do.

"My body went limp," he said. "I really couldn't move. I had to grasp what had just happened."

He had told himself as a young boy that someday he would win the Heisman Trophy. When he committed to being a defensive player at Michigan, he said, "that dream kind of left."

But in a season when all sorts of improbable dreams seemed to be coming true, Woodson's was alive again. In a vote that seemed to be a shock only in the state of Tennessee, Woodson was awarded the Heisman in New York City on December 13, exactly three months after the opening-game kickoff.

In September, it had appeared Peyton Manning would be given the Heisman by acclamation. He had been lauded for giving up the chance to turn pro and returning to Tennessee for his senior year. Then he led the Vols to a 10-1 season and an Orange Bowl match-up with Nebraska. He was smart, poised, a winner. His father, Archie, had finished third in the vote in 1970 behind two other quarterbacks, Jim Plunkett and Joe Theismann. This Heisman was supposed to be partly for him, too. But in this unlikely season, the Mannings ran second.

Woodson's game-breaking performance against Ohio State had clinched it. It almost had to be something as dramatic as that because of the impossibility of comparing offensive and defensive performances. Manning passed for 36 touchdowns and 3,819 yards during the season. In the Southeastern Conference championship game against Auburn he rallied his team from behind with four touchdown passes in a 30-29 victory. He did everything he was expected to do—except beat Florida. He never accomplished that in his career.

On the other hand, Woodson had 7 interceptions, 43 tackles, one sack, 11 pass receptions, 536 all-purpose yards, and 5 touchdowns, including one spectacular punt return. He also closed off half the field to opposing quarterbacks, who were simply intimidated out of throwing his way. How do you measure that in a statistic?

Marvin Jones, the Florida State linebacker, had finished fourth in the 1992 voting, and Warren Sapp, the Miami tackle, was sixth in 1996. That seemed to be as good as it would ever get for a defensive player.

But Woodson's mother, Georgia, knew differently. She had received a sign.

"During the Ohio State game, I asked God for a sign that Charles would win," she said. "Just then he made the punt return. That was the sign He gave me."

"This is sports history," said Marcus Ray, his closest friend on the team. "Now the standard has been set for defensive players. Charles just took it to another level. He told me before the season began, 'Marcus, I'm going to win every award in God's power.'"

Still, if it hadn't been for the offensive part of his game, the chances are good Woodson would have finished as just another defensive also-ran. Instead, he followed Tom Harmon and Desmond Howard as the school's third Heisman winner.

The state of Tennessee reacted as if someone had desecrated Elvis' grave. Vols coach Phil Fulmer called the result "a travesty." Angry fans and newspaper editorial writers from Knoxville to Memphis did everything but demand a Congressional investigation. But it really wasn't even close. It was, in fact, like a presidential election from the 1920s. Manning held on to the Solid South, but Woodson swept every other part of the country. The final count was 1,815 votes to 1,543, while Woodson took 433 first-place votes compared to Manning's 282.

An interested observer to the finish was Ryan Leaf, the quarterback of Michigan's Rose Bowl opponent, Washington State. He finished third in the vote.

If Michigan's season had been improbable, Washington State's was more like miraculous. It was the Pac 10 version of Northwestern's run to the Rose Bowl in 1995. The Cougars had not been anywhere near a major bowl game for decades. They were the only team from either the Big 10 or Pac 10 who had never been to the Rose Bowl over the fifty-year course of the agreement between the conferences. (Arizona had never gone there, either, but had only been eligible since joining the conference in the 1980s.)

WSU had not been to the big game since 1931 when it lost to Alabama. In its entire history Wazzoo had only been to six postseason games. Under Mike Price the program had been rebuilt in the '90s. With Drew Bledsoe as quarterback in the first half of the decade, the team had won two lesser bowls. Bledsoe was a number-one draft pick and within a few years had taken the New England Patriots to a Super Bowl.

Leaf turned out to be a better-than-adequate successor. Price had recruited him out of Great Falls, Montana, an area not known for its deep pool of talent. There isn't a single 1-A program within the state. So from that angle, WSU looked like the big time times two. But Pac 10 schools usually load up with California kids. They like playing in pleasant climates. At nine of the ten conference schools, that's what they got. Wazzoo was the tenth. Pullman is in an agricultural region on the state's eastern border. It has hot summers which are compensated for by cold winters. Its stadium holds fewer than 40,000 people and its hold on tradition is tenuous. That presented recruiting problems for Price.

He had managed to build a wide-open offense around Leaf and a talented group of receivers. The offensive line was good enough to give Leaf a little time. That was all he needed. The 6-6 quarterback had the fastest set-up and release in the country. Scouts who had seen them both said that Leaf could be a better pro prospect than Manning on sheer physical ability.

The Cougars had been given a major break in the schedule. They drew UCLA, regarded as the best team in the conference, at Pullman in the first game. Leaf got WSU off to a big lead and a wild fourth-quarter UCLA comeback fell just short, 37-34. That set the pattern for the entire season. Not once had WSU been held short of 24 points, but five times they had given up 31 or more. They had beaten up on patsies like Boise State and Southwest Louisiana, but they had been forced into overtime by a so-so Arizona team. In their toughest road game, they were beaten by defending conference champion Arizona State, 44-31.

Michigan had been toppling giants all year. Now the roles were switched. They were ranked first, undefeated, with all the prestige and all the tradition. And a Heisman Trophy winner, too. The Wolverines were established as a touchdown favorite in the game and that seemed conservative.

Except for one thing. This was the Rose Bowl. And Pasadena was where Michigan's dreams went to die. Since 1969, when Schembechler took his first team out there, not much had gone right for Michigan. They were 3-9 in the game.

Bo had his first heart attack there in '69. An undefeated season was ruined by Stanford in '72. A 7-4 Washington team dropped them in '78. Southern California's Charles White scored a touchdown without the benefit of having the football in his hands, having fumbled it, in '79. Arizona State, making its first trip to the game, beat a fourth-ranked Michigan team in '87. Bo got entangled in his headset wires while protesting a holding call, fell sprawling on the sidelines, and then got an unsportsmanlike conduct call tacked on in his last game as coach in '90.

This was not fun. But it had always been the goal.

Moreover, this was to be the final game under the Big 10 contract. After the 1998 game, if the Big 10 or Pac 10 champion was ranked first or second, it would go to the Bowl Alliance Championship, wherever it was being held. If it had been in effect this year, Michigan would have spent the holidays in Miami, getting ready to play Nebraska in the Orange Bowl. And one year out of every four the championship game will be held in Pasadena, which could cut out both the Big 10 and Pac 10, the host for every Rose Bowl ever played.

"The first time a team from another conference plays in that game the Big 10 will regret the day it ever got into another agreement," says Schembechler. "For what it symbolizes, the Rose Bowl is irreplaceable. No other bowl comes close. It was a huge mistake to give it up. I never agreed with the idea that we should be playing for a championship. We will have lost so much more in terms of tradition."

Carr was willing to break with one tradition, though. In past years, the Michigan team had flown to California on Christmas Day. This time he wanted to give his players two full weeks to acclimate themselves to the West Coast and to practice on grass in warm weather. Maybe that wasn't the main reason Michigan had gone 3-9, but the coach wasn't going to miss a bet. Not at these stakes.

CHAPTER 25

Bad Numbers

Everyone on the Michigan side was confident this was to be one game for the whole pot. No number-one team in history ever had lost its ranking after winning a bowl game. But Michigan was wrong to rest its faith in bowls and polls.

Since their inception by the Associated Press (AP) in 1936, the polls had been more a source of rancor than accord. Especially since 1950, the first time United Press International (UPI) joined the selection process with its own picks, the polls had been ludicrously flawed. On the average of once every three seasons since then, they either could not agree on a champion or the results had only a casual relationship to reality.

In some years it seemed the voters were balloting on the basis of regional loyalty, or emotion, or what they wished had happened rather than what actually occurred on the field. Moreover, it was never made clear if they were supposed to be considering the record over an entire season, or merely which team they felt was best at any given point in time.

The final poll of 1997, for example, ranked UCLA ahead of Washington State—although they had both finished with 10-1 records and WSU won the game between them. The polls were slender reeds on which to rest any kind of expectations.

The rise of the bowl games in the 1930s first heightened public interest in the polls. Michigan had played in the first recorded bowl, the 1902 Rose Bowl. The game had been dreamed up, almost as an afterthought, by the Tournament of Roses committee in Pasadena. New Year's Day festivities had been going on there since 1890, promoting Pasadena as an earthly paradise where flowers bloomed all winter. There were floats and beauty queens and the chief attraction was a burro race. Everyone had a swell time, but over the years it was felt something more was needed.

So an invitation was forwarded to Michigan, which had come through a 10-0 season in 1901, its first under Fielding Yost. The Wolverines were matched, for reasons not quite apparent now, against Stanford, which was 3-1-2 against vastly inferior competition. The Rose Bowl people soon saw their error. Stanford was no match for the "Point-a-Minute" Michigan powerhouse and succumbed 49-0. The contest was called several minutes early when Stanford could no longer field a sufficient number of able-bodied players.

This cooled the concept of a Rose Bowl game for the next fourteen years. In 1916 they tried again, asking Brown to come out and play Washington State. This time things went better for the West Coast team, with the Cougars winning 14-0. After this, the Bowl settled into its familiar annual rhythm, with a top team from the eastern half of the country invited to Pasadena to play the champions of the Pacific Coast.

By the 1930s, the game was drawing almost 80,000 spectators. Other warm-weather cities began to wonder why they couldn't get in on the action. The same idea occurred almost simultaneously to organizers in Miami and New Orleans. Both the Orange and Sugar Bowls made their debuts on January 1, 1935. The Florida game could lure only 5,000 fans, even though hometown team Miami was hosting Bucknell. The Sugar Bowl did somewhat better, with another local team, Tulane, defeating Temple in front of 22,000 customers. In two more years, the Cotton Bowl started up in Dallas, and by the end of the decade, all three of these postseason games were attracting crowds of better than 30,000.

But the concept of a college championship game was an altogether foreign idea. Even the NCAA basketball tournament would not begin until 1939. There had been a few previous, desultory attempts at designating a national champion. Starting in 1924, the Rissman Trophy was awarded by a loosely drawn panel of "experts." It lasted only seven seasons, and when Notre Dame won it for the third time in 1930, it was retired. This inspired a group of former Notre Dame players to award a championship trophy honoring their late coach, Knute Rockne, who had died that year in a plane crash. The Rockne Trophy was handed out for five seasons, with undefeated Michigan teams winning it in 1932 and 1933.

With the rise of the bowls, however, the selection of the top teams to play in postseason games began drawing national attention. The AP, recognizing a strong feature for its subscribing sports pages, initiated a weekly poll among football writers to rank the college teams.

The first one appeared on October 20, 1936, with Minnesota ranked number one. This was not much of a surprise. The

Gophers had won nineteen games in a row and were acknowledged to be the best team in the Big 10, the toughest conference in
football. Although they would lose to Northwestern, Minnesota
finished the season as the undisputed number-one team. Since
Big 10 teams did not participate in bowls, that settled that.

Although there were mild disputes over the top choice, most
number-one teams were fairly clear-cut between 1936 and 1949.
Twelve of the fourteen selections in that span did not play in a
bowl game; eleven of them were Big 10 teams, Army, or Notre
Dame. In 1947, however, an imbroglio developed. Both Michigan
and Notre Dame finished their seasons undefeated. Notre Dame
was the defending champion and had led the balloting for all but
three weeks, when Michigan had been the pick. The Wolverines
had beaten common opponents by bigger margins, but two close
midseason games against Minnesota and Illinois seemed to
swing the voters toward Notre Dame. This was the peak of Notre
Dame's "subway alumni" era. It was the only college with a truly
national following. The Irish were also in the midst of a thirty-
nine-game streak without a loss. All of this colored the voting.
Notre Dame finished with 107 first-place votes and 1,410 total
points compared to 1,289 for Michigan.

But this was also the second year of the Rose Bowl pact
between the Big 10 and Pacific Coast conferences. For the first
time in forty-six years, Michigan headed back to Pasadena to play
in a bowl game. There they destroyed Southern California by the
same 49-0 score they had run up on Stanford in 1902. Notre
Dame had beaten the Trojans only by 38-7 during the regular
season. This added fuel to the dispute over which team should
rightly be called national champions. Passions ran so high that
the AP called for an unprecedented post-bowl-game vote.
Michigan won it easily, with 226 of 357 first-place votes. But the

wire service refused to change the original result and Notre Dame was crowned the "official" national champion. Michigan never recognized the validity of that title, however. Members of the 1948 Rose Bowl team, the last one Fritz Crisler coached, were in the stands at the 1998 game to celebrate the fiftieth anniversary of "their" championship.

"Fritz wanted that game so badly," All-American halfback Bob Chappuis recalled years later. "We had a tradition that before every game, everyone on the team had to sing something. Fritz gave us seven or eight choruses of 'Old King Cole' before the Rose Bowl. It really didn't matter what the song was. It was just so astonishing to hear him sing."

Some of the sting of the number-two finish was eased when Michigan also went through the 1948 season without a loss and won the AP title, with Notre Dame at number two. Not until forty-nine years had passed would Michigan occupy that perch again at the end of a season.

The 1947 dispute only set the stage for greater discrepancies. In 1950, the UPI began its poll of college coaches. Oklahoma finished the season as the national champion in both polls. But in a staggering upset, the Sooners were beaten by Bear Bryant's Kentucky team in the Sugar Bowl. Meanwhile, the number-four team, Tennessee, upended number three Texas in the Cotton Bowl. The Vols also had beaten Kentucky during the season. To most observers, this clearly meant that Tennessee deserved to be rated number one. But the AP and UPI held fast to the policy of no revisions after the bowls. Oklahoma was awarded a spurious official title.

The same thing happened in 1951, 1953, 1960, and 1964. The first-ranked team lost its bowl game each time but no change was allowed in the championship award. The outcry after the 1964 debacle, when Arkansas was deprived of the title in spite of a perfect season after Alabama lost its bowl game, was so vociferous that the AP finally mandated a change. From then on, the post-bowl vote was the one that counted. All the members of that snubbed Arkansas team, including future Super Bowl coach and owner, Jimmy Johnson and Jerry Jones respectively, had championship rings made. They refer to themselves as members of a national-championship team. That is not, however, how the "official" record reads.

The UPI stubbornly adhered to its policy of no post-bowl revisions until 1973, when it became too ridiculous to continue. The UPI blindly gave Alabama its number-one ranking even after it was beaten by Notre Dame, the AP's number-one team, in the Sugar Bowl. Since then, both polls have factored in bowl results. But at least six teams were deprived of championships and two others were forced to share theirs undeservedly while the former rule was in force.

There were other split decisions, too. Because the UPI was a coaches poll, it was determined that no one would vote for a team that was on suspension by the NCAA. This meant that in 1957 Auburn, at a perfect 10-0, won the AP award, while Ohio State, at 9-1, got the UPI award. Again in 1974, Oklahoma (11-0-0) ruled the AP and Southern California (10-1-1) the pristine UPI.

There were also years in which the voters simply could not agree. In 1954, both Ohio State and UCLA finished the year unbeaten. Under the normal course of events, the teams would have met in a historic Rose Bowl. Unfortunately, the Pacific Coast Conference had enacted a short-lived no-repeat bowl rule. Ohio State pounded on a weak Southern California team in the bowl game, while UCLA sat home. The AP voted for the Buckeyes; the UPI chose the Bruins.

In 1965, previously unbeaten Michigan State was upended by UCLA in the Rose Bowl. The AP chose to elevate Alabama, even though it had an earlier loss and tie, ahead of the Spartans in its final poll. The UPI stuck with MSU.

Then in 1978 came one of those absurdities that only the football polls find logical. Alabama and Southern California played in September, with the Trojans winning, 24-14. Both teams finished the season with one loss and both won their bowl games. The AP determined this made Alabama the champion, while the UPI stuck with USC. Clearly, many AP participants were voting for Bear Bryant out of respect and sentiment. Many of them also seemed to believe that the early-season result should be discounted because at the end of the year Alabama was the better team. Under the hazy rules governing the vote, they were entitled to do so, idiotic as it may have been.

After that odd split decision, there followed an eleven-year string of unanimity. It was broken only in 1990 when the AP chose Colorado and the USA Today/CNN poll (which had supplanted UPI among the coaches) picked Georgia Tech. Again in 1991 the AP went for Miami and USA Today/CNN for Washington. Aside from those two seasons, however, there had been accord in picking a champion for twenty years.

The bowl games also had reshaped their selection policies to increase the chances that a clear-cut champion would emerge. There was some hope that a more coherent era had arrived in college football. Michigan, at least, was lulled into an assurance that common sense would prevail.

A few weeks before the games were played, Nebraska's coach, Tom Osborne, had announced his retirement. Since taking the job in 1973, he had compiled a remarkable record. Each of Osborne's teams had gone to a bowl game and twenty of them were major bowls. Criticized in the early '90s, after losing seven straight bowl games and failing to defeat any team ranked higher in the polls, he had answered with two straight perfect seasons. He won back-to-back national championships in 1994 and 1995.

Osborne could be a little short with the media and had no patience for what he regarded as dumb questions. But in Nebraska he was treated worshipfully. Even questions arising over his use of players with questionable academic and even criminal records did not diminish his luster. He was also enormously respected by his fellow coaches, who often voted their sentiment in national polls. Osborne's retirement became a wild card.

So were the TV networks. "You can't fight the networks," Schembechler had complained, and he was right. They called the tune, set the times, often dictated the match-ups in college football. CBS had invested a good deal of money and energy in promoting the Orange Bowl between Nebraska and Tennessee as the true championship game. It had been designated as such before the season even began by the Bowl Alliance. But no one had counted on a Big 10 team, bound to the Rose Bowl, coming into the holidays with the number-one ranking. That was enormously annoying at CBS. They were not going to let ABC, which broadcast the Rose Bowl, steal its thunder. CBS would do everything in its power to convince the public that the real championship would be decided on its air.

So as New Year's Day approached, an emotional retirement and a network's chest-pounding was altering a presumably set equation.

CHAPTER 26

The Subject Was Roses

No other stadium compares to it. Situated in the Arroyo Seco at the base of the San Gabriel Mountains, it is the most magnificent setting of any athletic facility in America. The Rose Bowl was built here in 1923 and has almost doubled in size since then. Officially, it seats 98,252, but only once since 1965 has it attracted fewer than 100,000 spectators.

Only the greatest are invited to play here. Since January 1, 1947, that has been defined as the champion of the Big 10. But before that Harvard had come. Knute Rockne's Notre Dame. Johnny Mack Brown had gone from playing quarterback for Alabama to playing a cowboy star in the movies. O.J. Simpson had run to glory here and so had Archie Griffin. Bob Griese had led Purdue to its only Rose Bowl victory in 1967.

It is an aging place, with corridors too narrow and locker rooms too small. The facilities of the 1920s, no matter how often they are upgraded, can't handle the demands of the 1990s. But there is no place like it. No other game has quite the same resonance.

"I sat in the stands all by myself when they first took us there," says Dhani Jones. "I closed my eyes, and I could almost hear the voices of all those great players who had been on the field. It was like they were calling to me."

Sam Sword recalled the great Michigan stars of the past. "Dan Dierdorf came out to talk to us," he says, "and I know Reggie Mackenzie. They had been on Rose Bowl teams here. And now I was going to do something that they never had the chance to do. I was going out there to play for a national championship for Michigan."

Tai Streets was alone with his thoughts, too. The kid from Chicago's South Side had enjoyed the season. He had made big touchdown catches against Notre Dame, Iowa, and Wisconsin— all of them tough games. It had been everything he dreamed about when he had chosen to come to Michigan. Almost. But a series of nagging injuries had plagued him in the final part of the year. He had been blanked in the Penn State and Ohio State games. No catches for the team's first deep option. And it bothered him.

"I pride myself in studying the game," he says. "My hero is Jerry Rice. And I learned from watching him that catching the ball and running are only a part of it. The other part is preparation. You have to learn about defenses, recognize their tendencies, not tipping off what you are going to do. It's much more than the average fan sees.

"A good receiver [has] to be thinking right along with his quarterback. I pride myself on doing that. And I also want the ball in my hands. I knew that I was being a part of history with this team. But I felt that I had more to accomplish."

Streets had not been a big college football fan. He was a receivers fan.

"I pulled for Rocket Ismail at Notre Dame and Desmond Howard," he says. "That's one of the big reasons I came here. Because it was Howard's school. And I loved the Chicago Bears. That's another thing that made this season so much fun for me. We played defense like those Bears teams in the '80s. I fed off that. Our defense would get a sack or an interception and I'd get all pumped up. We'd be ignited. Everything we did on the field played to our defense.

"I played all the sports when I was growing up. That's a big change even in these few years. You go to the fields in Chicago, around 114th Street where I grew up, and there's nobody playing ball there anymore. It's real rough around there. My mom didn't like the idea of me playing football at all. I came out as a running back as a freshman in high school and broke my ankle. My mom told me to stick to basketball and track. But the coach sat down with her and talked her into letting me come back. I mean, that's how close I came to giving this up. If the coach hadn't cared about me enough to back me up, I'm pretty sure I'd have done what my mom wanted. That's how life is, I guess.

"I didn't much care for the trip out to California. I'm not much for flying, if you know what I'm saying. We'd gone out to Colorado the year before and that was about as far as I wanted to go. I look on the schedule for this year and see we got a game in Hawaii and I don't know how I'm going to handle being over water for that long a time.

"But once I was out there, it was fine. Russell Shaw took a bunch of us on a ride through his old neighborhood. Down in L.A., in South Central. He showed us where he'd grown up and all the time I was thinking about 114th Street. We came a long way out of there. So I just sat in the empty stadium at the Rose Bowl that first day and thought that it's all like a picture postcard here and [tried] to visualize myself having a big game on that field."

There was a time when the Rose Bowl trip had been almost routine for Michigan fans. Three in a row between 1977 and 1979. Ten times in seventeen years.

But four years had gone by since the last trip and a deep hunger had grown in Michigan. Travel agents in the state had run through their ticket allotments quickly and many of the faithful had flown out to California on the chance of picking something up after arrival. But they were bucking the wide-eyed crowds from Washington State, who also were trying to snap up everything in sight. Brokers in Los Angeles could not recall a tougher ticket for this game.

Ira Jaffe, who gives the gourmand tailgate parties under the tent, had picked up his tickets and flown his family to Palm Desert. It was a chance to spend time together before driving to Pasadena for the game.

"I think I'd seen a game in 1947," Jaffe says. "I'd have been eight years old then, and I'm pretty sure I remember my dad talking about going to a game that year. Anyhow, I like to think that I actually saw that team play.

"The funny thing is that after going to all those games and being such a big Michigan fan, I wound up at the Massachusetts Institute of Technology. But every Sunday I'd phone home and talk about yesterday's game with my dad. He'd tell me about the big plays and the bad call somebody made on third down. Every Sunday during the football season we were on the phone together.

"I lost my dad when I was nineteen, away at school. That was tough. So the morning before we were heading to Pasadena I went out for my morning run and I had a tape that Mike Whorf at WJR made several years ago about great moments in Michigan football history. I'm running and listening to "The Victors," and I started thinking about my dad and how happy he would have been to be going to this game. And I started to cry. I'm singing and crying all at the same time.

"Then I went back to the hotel and I tried to tell my wife and my daughter about what had happened. Now I'm crying all over again. And they start to cry. But I look on this as part of my family's heritage. Here we were all together and it was such a happy time.

"We had started to wonder if it was over. All those four-loss seasons. The joy of being a power was gone. Now all of a sudden it was back. It was like a gift. I was going with the people who were the dearest to me in the world to watch the team of my childhood play in the biggest game I'd ever seen. And it was at the Rose Bowl."

At 5:00 P.M. Michigan time, with the darkness of winter already settling in, the bright California sun came streaming from the television into living rooms across the state. The final act of this story was about to begin.

CHAPTER 27

January 1. Michigan 21, Washington State 16

"When I was a kid, I cried when my team lost. Now I cry when my team wins."

GORDON GOLD,
Michigan graduate, after the Rose Bowl.

There had been nervous apprehension before the Ohio State game. Everyone understood what was at stake then, and the enemy was well known. The feeling now was harder to define. Yes, this was the Rose Bowl, where bad things happen. Yes, this game was for everything. But who knew anything about Washington State? This was a journey into the unknown. And what you don't know can't hurt you, right?

Actually, the teams had met three times before, all of them at Ann Arbor. Michigan had won all three games. Just four years ago they had taken care of the Cougars easily, 41-14, and Mike Price had been their coach for that one. So why worry? But it became apparent quickly that this was not going to be a 41-14 day.

On his third possession of the game, starting with good field position at the Michigan 47, Leaf took the Cougars right in. Six plays, a 15-yard scoring strike to Kevin McKenzie and just like that, it's 7-0.

The Michigan offense again seemed to be flailing, unable to find traction. Just as Ohio State did, WSU was containing the short passes and bringing up its linebackers to stop the run. Three Michigan possessions went nowhere, and as the second quarter began here came Leaf again.

Starting at his own 23, he hit Shawn McWashington for 22 yards. Then he found his top receiver, Chris Jackson, for 35 more. Now the Cougars were down at the Michigan 14, getting ready to move in for a forbidding two-touchdown lead. The 30,000 Michigan fans, most of them bunched in the stands in a maize and blue squadron, pleaded with the defense to make its stand now. A running play gained 2. Then Leaf dropped back, looking into the end zone.

But with the season teetering, it suddenly became Woodson Time once more. Just as he had against Ohio State, Woodson saw the pattern, leaped in front of the receiver, and had his eighth interception of the year. Disaster had been averted.

Still Michigan couldn't move. Three plays and a punt. In four possessions, they had managed just 68 yards in offense. Griese was 6 for 9 but they were all dink passes. He simply was not moving with any consistency or force.

The interception seemed to have awakened the defense, though, and it sacked Leaf for the second time of the game after the Michigan punt. Woodson brought back the ensuing WSU punt 15 yards and a penalty took the ball near midfield, Michigan's best starting point of the day. Griese went back to pass for the tenth time, but there would be no dink this time. Instead, he spotted Streets roaring down the middle of the field, behind the defense. He hit him in stride for a 53-yard strike, and Michigan had tied it up, 7-7.

If Leaf and the Cougars seemed temporarily stunned by the interception and touchdown, they had overcome their surprise by half time. Starting at his own 1 in the third quarter, Leaf brought his team 99 yards in 10 plays. He made it look shockingly easy against a defense that had given up almost no long drive all season—none this long, at least, since the Notre Dame game. Leaf was mixing it up. Three passes for 18 and 29 and 20 yards, then a 14-yard burst by Shawn Tims and Wazzoo was back in front, 13-7.

Griese responded immediately. Six plays, short passes and runs, brought Michigan out to its own 42. Then once again he faded and let fly downfield to the streaking Streets. Another long touchdown strike, and Michigan had edged back in front, 14-13.

The guy who couldn't throw long was giving a pretty good impersonation of a bomber. Streets, who had sat in the stands a few days before and envisioned himself playing well, had made the vision reality.

"His entire career, Brian had been hearing what he couldn't do," said Carr. "I think we all just got tired of hearing it."

He wasn't through, either. With the Cougars finally forced to respect his arm and fall back on defense, Griese led the Wolverines on a masterful, ball-control drive. It took 14 plays to march the 72 yards. All were either the standard, maddening short passes or quick openers with Williams or Floyd carrying the ball. Finally, from 23 yards out he found Tuman for the touchdown pass. It was the longest play of the drive, and Michigan was now in control, 21-13.

Once more, however, Leaf took the hit and kept coming. On a

drive in which he was sacked twice and forced to scramble almost every time, he still brought the Cougars close enough for a 48-yard field goal. More than eight minutes to play and Michigan was clinging to a 5-point lead. All Leaf wanted now was one more series of downs, a little bit of time.

Instead, on what may have been his finest drive of the season, Griese left him almost nothing. The drive resulted in no points, but it took 15 plays and seven and a half minutes. As Leaf watched in mounting agony, time slipped away from him. Four times Griese faced third-down plays to keep it alive and he made every one of them. He carried the ball himself on an 11-yard scramble on a third and 11. Then Woodson came in, pulled the ball down from a called option pass, and darted for 8 on a third and 7. Then it was a pass to Shaw, playing before his hometown crowd, on third and 6. Then Woodson again grabbing a pass on third and 8.

It was as precise and jewel-like as anyone had ever seen under conditions like these. When it finally stopped and Michigan's punt rolled dead at the WSU 7, Leaf had no time outs and 29 seconds to operate.

It was almost enough. He found Nian Taylor on a third-down heave and while Michigan screamed that he had blatantly pushed off from the defenders, WSU had the ball on the Michigan 47. The Cougars raced up the field as the clock stopped for the chains to be moved and tried again. Under 10 seconds now. Leaf hit his tight end, Love Jefferson, who lateralled to halfback Jason Clayton. He was brought down at the 26.

Less than 5 seconds remained as the Cougars again tried to set up at the line. The fans on both sides were up and screaming. This was one of the great Rose Bowl finishes, better than anyone had imagined. But Leaf would get one more shot, and images of Kordell Stewart and Michael Westbrook had not entirely been blotted out of the Michigan memory. This would be even worse if Leaf could pull it off.

He took the ball and spiked it to stop the clock. But no time was showing. The Michigan bench leaped up and then stopped as the officials rushed together to see if an extra second had inadvertently been run off. Both benches stood in suspended animation. Then came the sign. It was over. Michigan had won 21-16.

"I didn't know whether to laugh or cry or scream or what," says Sam Sword.

"I'd never had a feeling like that before," says Streets. "Everything I had ever dreamed about as a kid had just come true."

"I felt like I was in the middle of *Field of Dreams*," says Dhani Jones. "All I could think of was 'Welcome to Paradise.'"

"All I remember is not knowing whether it was over or not," says Carr. "Not knowing whether we could start to celebrate or if we had to go through one more play. For a few seconds, it was torture."

High above the stadium floor, in the ABC broadcast booth, Keith Jackson had an announcement to make. Turning slightly to Bob Griese, his partner and longtime friend, Jackson said: "The MVP, do we know who it is? Well, I'm standing beside his proud daddy."

Griese, struggling hard to get the words out, responded: "You about lost me, Keith."

"You want to go and cry, go ahead," Jackson said. Then the camera focused on the press box and there was Griese turning to hold his wife in a long, tearful hug. The season in which he had to play the neutral observer was over. Now he was like any other father, bursting with pride at what his son had done.

"You guys got me crying," said Jackson, a catch in his voice.

Brian, upon hearing that he had won the award, simply smiled and said: "I thought it should have gone to Tai Streets.

"All I ever wanted to do was contribute to this team and be a part of something special. I'm happy to be in the shadow of Ryan Leaf and just play my game. Today, my game came out on top."

His teammates clustered about him and began their chant: "It's great to be a Michigan Wolverine." Everest had been climbed, at last.

"The Victors" was playing once again, and in the stands old friends embraced, parents and children sang the words together.

"Hail to the Victors, Champions of the West."

CHAPTER 28

After the Miracle

Mike Price was convinced. The Washington State coach had seen enough.

"They made the plays they had to make when they had to make them," he said. "That's the mark of a champion, and they are the national champions. No question. They've got my vote."

"We've beaten everyone that was on our schedule," said Griese, in the postgame interview. "What more can you ask of us?"

When the telecast went off the air on New Year's night, ABC had anointed Michigan as champions. But there was one more game to play.

When CBS came on the air to begin its telecast of the Orange Bowl the following night, the network made it clear that the championship, in their opinion, was still an open question. Undefeated Nebraska should have a claim equal to Michigan's.

Tennessee gave the Cornhuskers a game for about a half and trailed 14-3 at the break. But Peyton Manning could never get untracked against a relentless Nebraska rush. In the second half the Tennessee defense crumpled against the deadly Nebraska option.

Three straight times at the start of the third quarter, Nebraska came down the field for touchdowns. It was now 35-9, and the issue no longer in doubt. But Nebraska knew the quickest way to a high ranking in the polls was to keep pouring it on. With a thoroughly beaten opponent facing them, Nebraska kept its first offensive unit in for the fourth quarter. Once more it drove in for a score, making it 42-9. The Vols, with Manning out of the game, finally were able to go in for a meaningless touchdown with seconds left in the game. The final count: Nebraska 42, Tennessee 17. It had been an impressive whomping of a team with a quarterback who had been rated the best in the country.

The AP media poll stuck with Michigan. But the coaches in the USA Today/CNN balloting chose Nebraska. It was the first time in the history of the polls that a number-one team had lost the ranking after winning its bowl game.

There were many reasons that could be given in justification of the unprecedented selection.

Six of the teams Michigan had beaten during the season lost their bowl games. Ohio State and Penn State, which had seemed so formidable within the Big 10, were beaten decisively. Nebraska, on the other hand, had given Fiesta Bowl winner Kansas State its only loss of the season and also defeated Washington, which had run all over Michigan State.

Nebraska had stopped Manning cold while Michigan had been hanging on for dear life at the end against Leaf. While there was some dispute over who was the better quarterback, Manning was chosen first in the subsequent NFL draft.

Nebraska did have several soft touches in its schedule and had defeated Missouri only on a seemingly illegal fluke. Still, Colorado had been voted in as national champions by the AP in 1990 even though it had only beaten Missouri when the game officials fouled up and gave the Buffaloes five downs on a critical touchdown drive.

Moreover, the coaches frequently looked out for their own. In 1993, for example, Florida State's Bobby Bowden was voted into the championship despite having lost its regular-season game to Notre Dame, the number-two team, which finished with the same record. The coaches seemed to feel it was Bowden's time. And a lot of them simply didn't like Notre Dame's Lou Holtz.

So the retiring Tom Osborne may have been given one more award for his trophy case on the reasoning that he had paid his dues in overtime while third-year coach Lloyd Carr had not.

Whatever. If there was any consolation it is that most reference books in listing the number-one team give priority to the AP poll, either listing it first or not including USA Today/CNN at all.

Nor did the split decision mitigate the celebration in Ann Arbor. There was a parade through the city's frigid January streets and in a rally at Crisler Arena the trophy was presented to the team's co-captains, Mayes and Jensen.

"That to me was the peak," says Jensen. "To see everybody standing up and singing 'The Victors' when they brought out the trophy. That was something I'll never forget. Then I went back to my high school in Clawson and they raised a championship banner there. That's why you come to a school like Michigan, to have the chance at moments like that."

The players, in fact, seemed to accept the co-championship with good grace. They had both finished 12-0; they were not allowed to play each other. So why not share it? Under the formula adopted by the NCAA for 1998 to determine the top two teams for the Alliance Bowl, Michigan, however, would have finished at number one.

Woodson, to absolutely no one's surprise, decided to leave school early and enter the draft. He ruffled a few feathers at some postseason banquets when his serene self-confidence was mistaken for arrogance. But he ended up as the fourth player chosen and went to the Oakland Raiders.

Griese, who had chosen by the slimmest of margins to return for the 1997 season and not to end his football career, was taken by Denver as the fourth quarterback pick in the draft. Only Manning, Leaf, and Eastern Michigan's Charlie Batch went higher. The possibility of such a pick would have been ludicrous less than a year before. When a scout for the Detroit Lions was quoted as being less than impressed by Griese's talents, Carr reacted as if he had been personally attacked.

"I may have overreacted a little," he says, "but after watching what he did for us that season, I don't know how anyone could question Brian Griese's abilities ever again."

In June, Carr was given a long-term contract calling for an annual salary of $675,000. Not a voice was raised in dissent.

By that time, with spring practice over, the returning Michigan players were almost writhing in anticipation.

"We know we're not going to surprise anybody," says Jensen. "As much as they had prepared for us in the past just because we were Michigan, it's going to be even more because we are the national champions. This is really going to be fun."

Sam Sword was looking forward to his first trip into Notre Dame. "We didn't play them at all my first two years and we had them at home last season," he says. "Now we're going down there on a business trip and I'm itching for that. That's the challenge. To go down there with that Notre Dame mystique and try and take over their stadium. How can you get complacent? There are so many challenges when you play here."

Tai Streets looks nervously at the wide expanse of blue on the map that separates the mainland from Hawaii, where Michigan will close its season.

Dhani Jones likes the idea of sitting in the stands at the Fiesta Bowl in January, just as he did in Pasadena, and thinking about the legacy of the past.

Ira Jaffe gets his tent out of storage. Howard King meets with his spotters and starts poring over the right pronunciations for this year's opponents. Longtime ticket holders renew their orders and look for the possibility of getting more. Entering freshmen grasp their first batch of season tickets and prepare to join the long march of tradition.

"I met Chuck Noll right after he won his third SuperBowl with the Steelers," said Carr. "I asked him about challenges, and he held up his hand to show me the latest ring. 'That's an antique now,' he said. That's the attitude we've got to have. As great as our season was, it's part of history now."

It is all about to begin again.

	Michigan	Opponents
First Downs	243	142
Rushes-Yards	558-2,188	386-1,068
Passing Yards	2,539	1,531
Pass Attempts-Completions	209-331	162-327
Interceptions	23	6
Fumbles Lost	12	4
Sacks-Yards	30-210	26-173
Time of Possession	389:43	330:17
Return Yardage	686	446
Penalties-Yards	83-662	77-644

	Rushing	Receiving	Total
Howard	937	276	1,213
Thomas	549	219	768
Streets	0	476	476
Williams	266	181	447
Tuman	0	437	437
Floyd	279	83	362
Shaw	0	284	284
Woodson	21	238	259
Shea	0	85	85
McCall	41	32	73
Campbell	0	61	61
Griese	21	28	49
Jackson	41	0	41
Knight	0	30	30
Schanski	25	0	25
Bryant	0	18	18
Wright	0	17	17
Ford	12	0	12
Dreisbach	7	0	7
Smith	5	0	5
Roth	0	1	1
Brady	-14	0	-14

MICHIGAN IN THE 1990'S

1990 Coach: Gary Moeller

Sept. 15	@Notre Dame	L 24-28
Sept. 22	UCLA	W 38-15
Sept. 29	Maryland	W 45-17
Oct. 6	@Wisconsin	W 41-3
Oct. 13	Michigan State	L 27-28
Oct. 20	Iowa	L 23-24
Oct. 27	@Indiana	W 45-19
Nov. 3	@Purdue	W 38-13
Nov. 10	Illinois	W 22-17
Nov. 17	Minnesota	W 35-18
Nov. 24	@Ohio State	W 16-13
Jan. 1	Mississippi (Gator Bowl)	W 35-3

9-3 AP Ranking 7

1991 Coach: Gary Moeller

Sept. 7	@Boston College	W 35-13
Sept. 14	Notre Dame	W 24-14
Sept. 28	Florida State	L 31-51
Oct. 5	@Iowa	W 43-24
Oct. 12	@Michigan State	W 45-28
Oct. 19	Indiana	W 24-16
Oct. 25	@Minnesota	W 52-6
Nov. 2	Purdue	W 42-0
Nov. 9	Northwestern	W 59-14
Nov. 16	@Illinois	W 20-0
Nov. 23	Ohio State	W 31-3
Jan. 1	Washington (Rose Bowl)	L 14-34

10-2 AP Ranking 6

1992 Coach: Gary Moeller

Sept. 12	@Notre Dame	T 17-17
Sept. 19	Oklahoma State	W 35-3
Sept. 26	Houston	W 61-7
Oct. 3	Iowa	W 52-28
Oct. 10	Michigan State	W 35-10
Oct. 17	@Indiana	W 31-3
Oct. 24	Minnesota	W 63-13
Oct. 31	@Purdue	W 24-17
Nov. 7	@Northwestern	W 40-7
Nov. 14	Illinois	T 22-22
Nov. 21	@Ohio State	T 13-13
Jan. 1	Washington (Rose Bowl)	W 38-31

8-0-3 AP Ranking 5

1993 Coach: Gary Moeller

Sept. 4	Washington State	W 41-14
Sept. 11	Notre Dame	L 23-27
Sept. 25	Houston	W 42-21
Oct. 2	Iowa	W 24-7
Oct. 9	@Michigan State	L 7-17
Oct. 16	@Penn State	W 21-13
Oct. 23	Illinois	L 21-24
Oct. 30	@Wisconsin	L 10-13
Nov. 6	Purdue	W 25-10
Nov. 13	@Minnesota	W 58-7
Nov. 20	Ohio State	W 28-0
Jan. 1	North Carolina State (Outback Bowl)	W 42-7

8-4 AP Ranking 21

1994 Coach: Gary Moeller

Sept. 3	Boston College	W 34-26
Sept. 10	@Notre Dame	W 26-24
Sept. 24	Colorado	L 26-27
Oct. 1	@Iowa	W 29-14
Oct. 8	Michigan State	W 40-20
Oct. 15	Penn State	L 24-31
Oct. 22	@Illinois	W 19-14
Oct. 29	Wisconsin	L 19-31
Nov. 5	@Purdue	W 45-23
Nov. 12	Minnesota	W 38-22
Nov. 19	@Ohio State	L 6-22
Dec. 30	Colorado State (Holiday Bowl)	W 24-14

8-4 AP Ranking 12

1995 Coach: Lloyd Carr

Aug. 26	Virginia (Pigskin Classic)	W 18-17
Sept. 2	@Illinois	W 38-14
Sept. 9	Memphis	W 24-7
Sept. 16	@Boston College	W 23-13
Sept. 30	Miami (Ohio)	W 38-19
Oct. 7	Northwestern	L 13-19
Oct. 21	@Indiana	W 34-17
Oct. 28	Minnesota	W 52-17
Nov. 4	@Michigan State	L 25-28
Nov. 11	Purdue	W 5-0
Nov. 18	@Penn State	L 17-27
Nov. 25	Ohio State	W 31-23
Dec. 28	Texas A&M (Alamo Bowl)	L 20-22

9-4 AP Ranking 17

BACK ON TOP

1996 Coach: Lloyd Carr

Aug. 31	Illinois	W 20-8
Sept. 14	@Colorado	W 20-13
Sept. 21	Boston College	W 20-14
Sept. 28	UCLA	W 38-9
Oct. 5	@Northwestern	L 16-17
Oct. 19	Indiana	W 27-20
Oct. 26	@Minnesota	W 44-10
Nov. 2	Michigan State	W 45-29
Nov. 9	@Purdue	L 3-9
Nov. 16	Penn State	L 17-29
Nov. 23	@Ohio State	W 13-9
Jan. 1	Alabama (Outback Bowl)	L 14-17

8-4 AP Ranking 20

1997 Coach: Lloyd Carr

Sept. 13	Colorado	W 27-3
Sept. 20	Baylor	W 38-3
Sept. 27	Notre Dame	W 21-14
Oct. 4	@Indiana	W 37-0
Oct. 11	Northwestern	W 23-6
Oct. 18	Iowa	W 28-24
Oct. 25	@Michigan State	W 23-7
Nov. 1	Minnesota	W 24-3
Nov. 8	@Penn State	W 34-8
Nov. 15	@Wisconsin	W 26-16
Nov. 22	Ohio State	W 20-14
Jan. 1	Washington State (Rose Bowl)	W 21-16

12-0 AP Ranking 1

Index

A

ABC, 75, 76, 164
Adami, Zach, 20, 30, 97
admission standards, 60, 90
Alvarez, Barry, 133, 134
AP. *See* Associated Press
Associated Press poll, 59–60
    flaws, 157–58
    history, 159–63
    Michigan ranking, 10, 34, 35, 60,
        131
        for 1997 season, 81, 129, 178,
            179

B

Backus, Jeff, 20, 30
Banks, Tavian, 96, 98
Banks, Tony, 107
Barnett, Gary, 89, 90, 104
Battle, Bill, 85
Baylor University football, 45, 47
Berenson, Red, 40
Big House. *See* Michigan Stadium
Big 10 conference

Michigan in, 17, 35, 57, 92, 139
and Michigan State, 102, 103
national status of, 120, 139
and Northwestern, 90
and Paterno, 121
schedule of, 62
Big 12 conference, 7
Bledsoe, Drew, 154
Bollinger, Lee, 60–61, 68–69, 128–29
Boston, Glenn, 140, 144, 148
Bowl Alliance, 155, 164, 180
bowl games, 158–163, 164 (*See also*
    Rose Bowl)
Brady, Tom, 20, 30
Brown, Reggie, 130
Bruce, Earle, 139

C

Cameron, Cam, 78
Canham, Don
    as athletic director, 10–12, 14, 32
    retirement, 65, 66, 67–68
    Carr, Lloyd, 73, 91, 114–16
    career of, 21–22, 55, 57, 180
    coaching style of, 53–55 (*See also*

Carr, Lloyd, motivating team;
Carr, Lloyd, and players)
on defense, 25–26, 116
and family, 22–23
on Griese, 27, 75, 100, 115–16, 173,
180
on Michigan tradition, 54
and Moeller, 22, 31, 43
motivating team, 54, 92, 96, 127
November record of, 56, 114
and players, 55, 115, 130 (*See
also* Carr, Lloyd, coaching
style of; Carr, Lloyd, motivating team)
on pressure, 22, 23, 54, 57–58
on Rose Bowl, 175
on Woodson, 49
1995 season of, 54–56
1996 season of, 56–57
on 1997 season, 58, 72, 99, 134
on 1998, 181
Carr, William, 56
Carter, Anthony, 29
CBS, 164
Chappuis, Bob, 161
Chicago Bears, 126, 167
Cleary, Anthony, 121
CNN/USA Today poll. *See* USA
Today/CNN poll
college football, 9, 28 (*See also
under specific school names*)
bowl games and national rankings, 157–59, 159–63
coaches, 40, 42, 179 (*See also
under specific names*)
college rankings, 59. *See* Associated
Press poll; United Press
International poll; USA
Today/CNN poll
Collegiate Licensing Co. (CLC), 85
Collins, Todd, 39
Colorado, University of, football, 7,

25, 26, 27–28
Cook, Beano, 34
Cooper, John, 40, 62, 139
Cotton Bowl, 159
Crisler, Fritz, 9, 12, 65, 66, 161

D

Davies, Bob, 63
DeBord, Mike, 48
Deeds, Jay, 86–87
defensive players and Heisman
Trophy, 110–11, 152, 153
DeLisle, Tom, 145–46
Detroit Lions, 43, 180
Detroit media, 39
Detroit Tigers, 11, 14, 33, 114
Dreisbach, Scott, 18, 19, 55, 57
Duderstadt, James J., 67–68

R

Elbel, Louis, 3
Elliott, Bump, 10, 11, 14, 15
Excalibur (restaurant), 37, 38

F

Fab Five, 41–42
Falls, Joe, 36, 39
Feazell, Juaquin, 30
Feldman, Howard, 84–85
Fisher, Steve, 41, 42, 68, 69
Fleming, Robben, 66
Florida State University football, 29,
149
Floyd, Chris, 30, 145
football. *See* college football
football injuries, 130
Franklin, Denny, 15
Freehan, Bill, 40
Frieder, Bill, 41

Fry, Hayden, 95, 98
Fulmer, Phil, 153

G

Gantner, Fran, 125
Germaine, Joe, 144, 148
"Go Blue" banner, 6
Golden, Marshall, 28
Goss, Tom, 4, 69
Griese, Brian, 18–20, 30, 73–75
    calmness of, 72, 74, 98, 140
    as MVP, 175, 176
    and NFL draft, 180
    passing of, 27, 91, 96, 99, 134–35
    respecting opponents, 91, 121
    at Rose Bowl, 172–73, 174
    on Woodson, 49
Griese, Bob, 18, 73, 74
    covering son's games, 75–76, 175
Griese, Judy, 74
Grossman family, 83

H

Hanlon, Jerry, 34
Hannah, John, 102
Harbaugh, Jim, 114
Hayes, Woody, 10, 12, 137–39
Heisman Trophy, 48, 108, 110–11,
    151–53
Hendricks, Tommy, 72, 73
Herrmann, Jim, 21, 73, 81
    on players, 25, 48, 100
Hessler, John, 25, 26, 27
Holtz, Lou, 43, 179
Howard, Chris, 30, 47, 48–49
Huff, Ben, 30
Husband, John, 84
Hutchinson, Steve, 30

I

Illinois, University of, football, 31–32
Indiana University football, 77–79
Into Thin Air, 92
Iowa, University of, football, 95–96,
    98–100
Irons, Jarrett, 55

J

Jackson, Keith, 74, 76, 175
Jackson, Stanley, 144, 146
Jaffe, Ira, 4, 168–69
Jansen, Jon, 20, 72, 96–98, 148
    on national championship, 179,
        180
Jones, Dhani, 30, 79–81, 127–28
    at Rose Bowl, 166, 175
Jones, Marvin, 152

K

Kasischke, Lou, 92–93
Katzenmoyer, Andy, 144
King, Howard, 5–6
Kipke, Harry, 4
Knapp, Bob, 50, 51
Knight, Bobby, 77
Krakauer, Jon, 92, 93

L

Leach, Rick, 15, 114
Leaf, Ryan, 153, 154
    at Rose Bowl, 172, 173–75, 176
Lester, Dr. Mel, 4
Leuchtenburg, William E., 13

M

Madej, Bruce, 21
Mallory, Bill, 77
Manning, Archie, 18, 152

Manning, Peyton, 18, 48, 151–52, 177–78

Mason, Glen, 32, 117

Maviglia, Vincent, 38

Mayes, Eric, 61–62, 79

McQueary, Mike, 122–23, 126

Miami, University of, football, 60

Miami Dolphins, 18

Miami of Ohio football coaches, 12–13

Michigan, University of
  academics, 7, 18, 59, 60, 61
  alumni, 46, 61, 85, 86
  athletic department, 11, 32
  athletic department directors, 10–12, 65–69
  athletic standards, 40, 42, 69 (*See also* Michigan Way)
  basketball, 41–42, 68
  campus, 2
  colors, 85
  marching band, 3, 6, 97
  merchandise, 85–86
  presidents, 66, 67, 68–69 (*See also* Bollinger, Lee)
  research institution, 61
  sports program lure, 60
  stadium. *See* Michigan Stadium

Michigan, University of, football
  announcer, 5–6
  Army, games against, ix
  Associated Press poll ranking, 10, 34, 35, 60, 131
  for 1997 season, 81, 129, 178, 179
  Baylor, games against, 45, 47
  big plays of 1997 season, 72, 99, 108, 109, 145–47
  Big 10 standing, 17, 35, 57, 92, 139
  Carr as coach, 21–22, 54–57 (*See also* Carr, Lloyd)
  coaches, 9–10, 11 (*See also* Carr, Lloyd; Moeller, Gary;

  Schembechler, Bo)
Colorado, games against, 7, 25–28
defense, 25–27, 28, 81, 116, 167
  opponents dealing with, 91, 125–26, 133–34, 173
  strengths and weaknesses, 20–21
expectations, 6–7, 17, 22 (*See also* Michigan Way)
fans, 7, 46–47, 83–84
  enthusiasm of, 25–26, 71–72, 98
  expectations of, 22, 36
  loyalty of, x-xi, 84, 86
  memories of, 28–29, 87, 145–46, 168–69
  at Rose Bowl, 168
  student, 3–4, 128, 148
Florida State, game against, 29
history, x, 9–12, 14–15, 102–104 (*See also* Rose Bowl)
Illinois, games against, 32
Indiana, games against, 77–79
Iowa, games against, 95–96, 98–100
losing record, 10, 21, 22, 35
losing teams' reaction, 110
marketing, 10–11
media coverage, 21, 36, 39
Michigan State, games against, 34, 107–110
Michigan State rivalry, 101–102, 103
Minnesota, games against, 113–14, 117
Moeller as coach, 27–28, 34–35 (*See also* Moeller, Gary)
most points scored against team, 29
national champion title, 60, 160–61, 178, 179–80

Northwestern, games against, 55,
56, 81, 87, 89, 90–92
Notre Dame, games against,
62–63, 71–73, 180
November record, 114, 129
offense, 15
ball-control game of, 126,
134–35
problems with, 20, 79
and Woodson, 47–48, 49, 111
Ohio State, games against, 10, 15,
19, 144–48
Ohio State rivalry, 57, 137–40
Penn State, games against, 57, 121,
122, 125–27
players
and academics, 18, 60, 80
celebrating, 148, 176
and coaches, 14, 33, 55 (*See
also* Carr, Lloyd, and
players; Schembechler, Bo,
and players)
discipline required by, 61
and national champion title,
179
pressure on, 22, 35
problems of, 40, 74–75, 127
recruited from, 30
at Rose Bowl, 166, 167–68,
175–76
traditions' influence on, 61,
80–81, 96, 98
practice, 26, 127, 156, 166
pregame, 1–3, 4–5
preseason practice, 97–98
pressure, 22, 35–36 (*See also* Carr,
Lloyd, on pressure)
Purdue, game against, 56
quarterbacks, 18, 19–20 (*See also*
Griese, Brian)
recruiting, 12, 29–30
Rose Bowl trips, 57, 139, 155, 158,
160, 168
in 1998, 171–75
schedule, 17–18, 45–46, 62
Schembechler's influence, 13
Stanford University, game
against, 158
strengths and weaknesses, 20–21
student fans, 3–4, 128, 148
team, 25, 30, 115 (*See also*
Michigan, University of, football, players)
team concept, x, 27, 81
team preparation, 26, 127, 156, 166
television exposure, 61
tickets, 3–4, 11, 46, 69
tough games (1997 season),
71–73, 96, 98–100
tradition, x, 62
as asset, 54
on defense, 26, 116
as detrimental, 6–7
at game, 5, 6
influence of, 54, 62, 166
of winning, 9–10, 22, 56, 60–61
Virginia, game against, 55
Washington State, games against,
171–75
watershed games, 15, 27–28
winning tradition, 9–10, 22, 56,
60–61
Wisconsin, games against, 133–35
Michigan Dynasty, x, 6
Michigan Stadium
attendance records, ix, 17, 46, 138,
143
empty seats, 11
enlargement, 3–4
Michigan State University, 101–105
football, 34, 62, 101–105, 107–110
rivalry with Michigan, 101–102,
103
Michigan Way, x , 40, 42

Miller, Dee, 147

Minnesota, University of, football, 113–14, 117

Missouri, University of, football, 129

M Let's Go Blue, 85

Moeller, Ann, 37–38

Moeller, Gary, 31–36
    coaching, 33–36, 53, 89
    intoxication and dismissal, 28, 37–40, 42–43
    recruiting, 29, 30

Munn, Biggie, 102

N

national champion title
    with Bowl Alliance, 155–56, 164, 180
    from bowl games and polls, 120, 159, 160–63
    for 1997 season, 164, 177, 178–80

NCAA basketball finals, 41, 42, 159

Nebraska, University of, football, 60, 129, 163–64, 177–79

Neuheisel, Rick, 7, 27

NFL draft, 180

Northwestern University football, 55, 56, 87, 89–91, 104

Notre Dame, 59–60
    football, 62–63, 71–73, 159, 160, 180
    merchandise, 85–86

O

offensive linemen, 97

Ohio sports, 138

Ohio State University football, 62
    against Michigan, 10, 15, 19, 144–48
    rivalry with Michigan, 57, 137–40

Rose Bowl, 15, 103, 139, 140

Oosterbaan, Bennie, x, 10

Orange Bowl, 159, 164, 177–78

Orr, John, 41

Osborne, Tom, 163–64, 179

P

Pac 10 conference, 154

Parrish, Stan, 74, 134

Pasadena (California), 158

Paterno, Joe, 119, 120–22

Patrick, Van, 12

Payne, Rod, 55

Pearson, Pepe, 144

Penn State University football, 57, 62, 119–21, 122, 125–27

Perles, George, 40, 104

"Point a Minute" team, 9, 158

polls. *See* Associated Press poll; United Press International poll; USA Today/CNN poll

Powlus, Ron, 71, 72, 73

Price, Mike, 153, 154, 171, 177

Purdue University football, 18, 56

R

rankings. *See* Big 10 conference; Associated Press poll; United Press International poll; USA Today/CNN poll

Ray, Marcus, 28, 109–110
    and Ohio State game, 137, 140, 141, 148
    on team preparation, 127
    on Woodson, 50–51, 152–53

Revelli, James, 3

Rice, Jerry, 166

Rissman Trophy, 159

Roberson, Joe, 39, 40, 68–69

Roberts, Dave, 47
Rockne Trophy, 159
Rogers, Darryl, 102
Rose Bowl
    eligibility, 15, 103, 162
    history, 158, 160, 165–66
    Michigan, 10, 34, 132, 155, 168
    Michigan in 1998, 171–75
    Michigan-Ohio State rivalry, 15,
        103, 139, 140

S

Saban, Nick, 104, 108
Salsinger, H. G., ix-x
Sapp, Warren, 152
Schembechler, Bo
    as athletic director, 32, 41, 65–66
    as coach, 10, 12–13, 14–15, 35, 97
        (See also Schembechler, Bo,
        and players)
    confrontational style of, 14, 33
    and Detroit Tigers, 33, 67
    and Indiana University, 77
    and Moeller, 31–32, 33, 40, 43
    on 1997 season, x, 26, 134
    and players, 5, 14, 33 (See also
        Schembechler, Bo, as coach)
    and Michigan State rivalry, 103,
        104
    and Ohio State, 10, 138–39
    on polls and rankings, 131–32, 139
    on recruiting, 29, 61
    on Rose Bowl, 155–56
    today, 13–14
Schultz, Todd, 108, 109
Seder, Larry, 86
Shaw, Russell, 30, 167
Sherman, Matt, 98, 99
Slippery Rock, 5–6
Sousa, John Philip, 3

Southwestern Conference, 45
Sports Illustrated, 60, 148
sports licensing business, 85
Stanford University football, 158
Steele, Glen, 20, 140
Stewart, Kordell, 28
Streets, Tai, 19, 134, 166–68
    at Rose Bowl, 173, 175, 176
Sugar Bowl, 159
Swett, Rob, 30
Sword, Sam, xi, 127, 129
    on defense, 26
    on Notre Dame, 180–81
    and Rose Bowl, 166, 175
    on Wisconsin game, 133–34
    on Woodson, 117

T

tailgate parties, 4
Taylor, Daydrion, 30, 129–30
television networks sport coverage,
    164
Tennessee, University of, football,
    151–52, 153, 177–78
Thomas, Anthony, 47
Tufts University, 59
Tuman, Jerame, 27, 30

U

United Press International poll, 157,
    161, 162–63 (See also USA
    Today/CNN poll
universities. *See under state or city
    name*
UPI poll. *See* United Press
    International poll
USA Today/CNN poll, 129, 163, 178,
    179
U.S. News and World Report, 59

V

"The Victors," 3
Virginia, University of, football,
54, 55

W

Wangler, John, 15
Washington State University foot-
ball, 153–54, 171–75
Watkins, Sue, 85–86
Weathers, Andre, 146
Webber, Chris, 42
Weidenbach, Jack, 66–67, 68
White, Mike, 32
Williams, Josh, 147
Wingfield, Antonio, 140, 144
Wisconsin, University of, football,
133–35
Woodson, Charles, 20, 47–51
    as best player, 111, 117
    competitive drive of, 48, 50–51,
        107–108, 109
    competitors on, 98, 123, 140–41
    on defense, 26, 91–92
    and Heisman Trophy, 108, 110,
        111, 151, 152–53
    against Iowa, 98
    against Michigan State, 107–108,
        109, 110
    and NFL, 180
    offensive game of, 47–48, 49, 111,
        135, 153
    against Ohio State, 145, 146
    at Rose Bowl, 172, 174
    self-confidence of, 50–51, 111, 117,
        180
Woodson, Georgia, 50, 152

Y

Yost, Fielding, 9, 65, 66